TELL '38

TELL '38

'38

ROLF HOCHHUTH

Translated by Michael Roloff

LITTLE, BROWN AND COMPANY

Boston   Toronto

FIRST ENGLISH-LANGUAGE EDITION

Rolf Hochhuth's Basel speech appeared in 1977 in a private edition.
The author amended the notes and documents for the 1979 edition
published in Germany.

"Investigating the Beer Cellar Explosion" (slightly condensed) from
The Labyrinth: The Memoirs of Hitler's Secret Service Chief by Walter
Schellenberg. Translated by Louis Hagen. Copyright © 1956 by Har-
per & Row, Publishers, Inc. Reprinted by permission of Harper &
Row, Publishers, Inc., and Andre Deutsch.

Library of Congress Cataloging in Publication Data

Hochhuth, Rolf.
  Tell 38.

  Translation of: Tell 38.
  1. Hochhuth, Rolf—Political and social views.
2. Bavaud, Maurice, 1916-1941. I. Title. II. Title:
Tell thirty-eight.
PT2668.03Z47613   1984   943.086   84-10020
ISBN 0-316-36766-4

BP

Designed by Patricia Girvin Dunbar

*Published simultaneously in Canada
by Little, Brown & Company (Canada) Limited*

PRINTED IN THE UNITED STATES OF AMERICA

I

THE SPEECH

Dear Herr Regierungspräsident Burckhardt, friends, ladies and gentlemen: Getting slapped around and slapping back is a state of affairs I am rather used to. But to be honored, as I am here today, and to be overwhelmed with words of praise and with a handsome check, such generosity and unhypocritical goodwill presumes an attitude which I lack — where could I have acquired it?

When this city ennobled me in a like manner once before, I could accept it more easily because I did not stand in the auditorium of this old museum whose intimidatingly magnificent past almost makes me speechless. And at the same time — as the first non-Swiss — I did not have to express my gratitude for *the* prize which was also awarded to the great author of *Richelieu*! No, thirteen years ago I received this honor from a Baseler who was dealing in used bicycles, and as I was paying him, the man said — he had probably seen my photo on the occasion of the recent, somewhat too noisy performance of *The Deputy* — "Hi there, Herr Dürrenmatt."

"That's not me — that's who I used to be," I assured him. For we found out at once that even with our controversial name and as foreigners so many people welcomed us in Basel that I could not even begin to thank all those who are still alive. But I want to thank three Swiss in particular, of whom I only know one myself; and also thank a number of institutions in this republic

whose inhabitants have the right to hold referendums and to
have a police force — where else is this possible? — to whom
an *author* can express his gratitude. For this police force with
two hundred men half inside and half outside the theater protected and made possible the first performance of my piece outside Germany. The police are not like that everywhere! Not far
from here,[1] the police looked the other way, and consequently
the Basel truck which had transported the set there had its tires
slashed and canvas tarp tossed in the river. And I don't even
want to mention those locations where the police and the political parties did not even permit performances of this or of other
pieces of mine. This canton, after all, has as its president Dr.
Lukas Burckhardt, the incumbent who molds political opinion,
and who wrote me that if certain courts which regard themselves
as my creditors try to extort English pounds from me — thirty
or fifty thousand, I don't recall the exact sum — he would try
to help. No politician would even have *said* that anywhere else;
no one else said it anywhere else.

A German politician protected me openly only once, but he,
Thomas Dehler, has been dead for some time;[2] and only once
did a British politician, the Labour MP Professor Strauss, who
pushed through a resolution in Parliament eliminating British
theater censorship, which had been the law since 1737 when a
political comedy by Henry Fielding was prohibited. Because the
censor sought to prohibit my piece *Soldiers*, he himself was prohibited. London saw 122 performances of my play, and since
1968 Great Britain has been free of theater censorship.

In Basel even ordinary officials protect writers. When the
bailiff was prodded to try to prod 26,000 francs out of me, because I had allegedly written a disdainful letter to *The Observer*,
this Basel official said to me: "I read your play *Soldiers*. Why
don't you simply write them: I am standing on legalities." What

does that mean? I asked, and he replied: "I don't know exactly myself, but it helps." It did help. I can recommend it to everyone.

And three years ago when the Christian Democratic party in my native state of Hesse and Schleswig-Holstein brought charges against me for "inciting to riot" in my play *The Midwife*, the Basel official who called me to inform me let it be known that the judicial authorities in Bern regarded the charge as idiotic. "You aren't obliged to do this, but your countrymen want a statement," he explained, "do you wish to make one?" "Nothing against it," I replied, whereupon he suggested: "Well, why don't you simply type it yourself?" And left me alone in his office.

This imperturbability is so typical of Basel, this ironic pragmatism; this absence of the hysteria that afflicts so many of my fellow Germans, myself included, who like to assemble their crisis staffs so as to brainstorm at night, as if they could not sleep then and meet during the day. This attitude is a type of applied philosophy, is the attitude of the wise Erasmus carried over into everyday life. It is an unarrogant distancing from everything that believes itself to be good because it is new, to be revolutionary because it is loud, and significant because it has sold millions of copies. No one in Basel expressed this attitude as classically as did Herr Heuberger who, until his retirement, was in charge of the university lending library — an institution that lends with the same legendary patience as a bank on the Freien Strasse.

I needed an old issue of *Der Spiegel* but could not find that magazine at the university library. "I've heard," I said, "that the reading society collects volumes for the library." Herr Heuberger replied with truly oriental serenity: "Ah well, you know, *Der Spiegel* — we're familiar with it, but we don't collect it. We throw it out." Since then, this library, one of the most stimulating repositories of learning which I have ever had the honor or good fortune to exploit, has begun to collect *Der Spiegel*.

It was also at the University of Basel where a scholar of German literature first defended me on purely literary grounds. Others had already studied the historical foundations of my pieces, but Professor Heinz Rupp also investigated my dramatic techniques, my free rhythms, and it was he who brought my play *The Deputy* and myself as well to Walter Muschg, who allowed me to attend his advanced seminar for three semesters. On Monday, it will be eleven years since Muschg keeled over dead in the post office on Bruderholz-Allee — Monday, December 6, 1965. Muschg had actually delivered his own obituary three days earlier in his last seminar next door on Martinsgasse. There, prompted by a student's dissertation on poverty in the work of Gotthelf,[3] he presented a passionate argument that the realm of politics and sociology should not be off limits to poets and students of German literature. A doctoral candidate who had written on Wallenstein argued that, unlike aesthetics and philology, such trivial matters as wage disputes, poor houses, care of orphans, alcoholism, the plight of servants, and the sly tricks of lawyers, should not be of concern to scholars of German literature.

Muschg, the author of *Tragische Literaturgeschicte (The History of Tragic Literature)*, who rediscovered Gotthelf and who sought to establish the work of Hans Henry Jahnn and Alfred Döblin as classics, argued to the contrary. In the last of his great essays,[4] and again in his last seminar, he justified and even demanded, more radically than any other Swiss critic has, that writers adopt a political stance in their works, just as their fellow citizen do and as Muschg himself did when he served on the National Council during the war. His last words were tantamount to a declaration of war against the Frankfurt School, which enjoyed an almost absolute dominance at that time, and the mad "aesthetic" law it formulated: "The rudiments of meaning in poetical works, which are external to it [*das unabdingbar Nichtkünstlerische an der Kunst*]." The Frankfurt School introduced the custom (which has not died out with the school) into the Federal Republic of politically denouncing all those artists who did not "dissolve the social contract with reality," as Adorno demanded, so that they could pursue so-called autonomous art! As Adorno goes on to argue, "Anyone of a culturally conservative bent who demands that a work of art say something . . . for which we invoke the term 'statement' [*Aussage*] in German . . . is allying himself with the opposing political position against the hermetic work of art which is beyond any purpose [*zweckfern*]. . . ."

Walter Muschg, however, has shown that anyone who rejects this "hermetic, autonomous" glass bead game of abstraction that is "beyond any purpose" and chooses instead to practice art as a form of reality can easily link up with the tasks and ideas of the works of the Enlightenment, which had been almost completely buried by 1960. Muschg was the first to unearth again the table of laws inscribed by Lessing; he demands that the writer fight and forbids him to slink away from the arena of sociopolitical conflict into the so-called new world-fields and, as Muschg put it derisively, "the clever playfulness of poetry that has become objectless," that has playfully freed itself of any "fidelity to empirical reality, any responsibility toward the linguistic norm, and any reverence for organic form." Muschg leveled an accusation at the still powerful imitators and "camp followers of late expressionism" who, along with every "binding tradition," had also "tossed all ideology overboard"; Muschg accused them of making an antihuman attempt "to shatter the language of reality, while this reality grows beyond us to gigantic proportions, as in a nightmare, and is about to crush us."

With the help of the French existentialists, Muschg proposed that "after all the playful experimentation with language," we should once again draw on the "spiritual energies that lie dormant within a word" to make the word into "the tool of detonating thought."

It was only logical that the Frankfurt School, which taught two generations of German artists to despise the social milieu, the world around them, did not acknowledge those who set up or tear down this world; indeed, the Frankfurt School even denied that such individuals existed! It was also only logical that these students of the Frankfurt School, true to their upbringing, accused me time and time again of "personalizing conflicts" in my pieces as a result of my "ahistorical obsolete dramaturgy" (which is by no means my own but rather that of history) instead of letting this dramaturgy announce itself through the study of human beings caught up in historical processes! Again, it is only logical that Adorno's school has not brought forth any historians, not a single true expert, but rather countless interpreters of history.

How often I had cause to use Sartre's statement "There are no inhuman situations" against the disciples of this school, who in complete seriousness would find fault with me for still according the freedom to make decisions to some (although not all) individuals in my plays. These disciples were trained to march with firm tread to their master's dogma of the "abdication of the subject" (*Abdankung des Subjekts*)[5] to so-called anonymous forces.

Aside from natural ones, catastrophes have been caused only by man himself!

I discussed no question more intensively with Karl Jasper and also with Hannah Arendt (who wrote about it in *The Banality of Evil*) than that of the responsibility of the individual in an age of flight from responsibility, an age which has been marked by

Befehlsnotstand (the state of emergency created in an individual when ordered to perform an immoral act).

The Adorno school pointed out the emergency exits for this flight from responsibility for one's actions; yet it did so without, however, being so consistent as to transfer the Frankfurt classrooms over to the courtrooms where the Auschwitz trial was being held, to demand the release of the murderers on the stand. According to the Frankfurt School, those who were being tried there were "will-less recipients of orders, freely interchangeable character masks and puppets of so-called faceless authorities"!

I was immune to the influence of this school which dominated almost entirely during the postwar period with its ideology of the incapacitation of the individual, and for this immunity I have to thank the basic maxims of the man from Basel who in all his works based himself on "the only cornerstone that we still have, the long-suffering, striving and active human being, what he is and was always like and will always be." Yes, for this I have to thank Jakob Burckhardt who programmed me more lastingly than any, but any other author.

Ordinarily I would not risk talking to — of all people — the citizens of Basel about Burckhardt, but cannot conceive of myself without the coincidence that I, the personally unscathed observer of the war and of the postwar tragedies, who grew up in a scarcely bombed small German town (which, after the defeat, became a border crossing between the American and Russian zones of occupation), found for myself a historian as interpreter of these otherwise undecipherable events. And the attitude of this historian, no matter how merry it might be otherwise, was chiefly determined, once he had lost his mother at the age of twelve, by "a sense for the great fragility and uncertainty of everything earthly."

I came upon his letters and reflections in the house of the parents of my first childhood friend, who is now a physician as

his father had been, and I came upon them in those years when
the life-determining decision are made in each and every spiritual being. It may be shameful to confess but I must admit that
all I have done in the thirty years since those early days is to
broaden my knowledge. I have not changed my view of "men
within history," which is the subtitle of the always fascinating
book about Burckhardt by Löwith, whose student I still was in
Heidelberg. Löwith's work (published in Switzerland of course,
in Lucerne) closes with the admonition which should be made
to each and every young German: that that horrible compatriot
who called himself his country's misfortune — and who truly
was it! — was never wiser than in Turin where on the Dionysian
note to his "honored Jakob Burckhardt" he relinquished the
claim to be a teacher of humanity to the moderating man from
Basel.

For we must love Burckhardt as much for what he reveals to
us as for what he spares us. For example, in accordance with
his teacher Ranke, whose godforlorn skepticism he so fortu-
nately lacks, he has a passion for art, just as, compared to
Mommsen, he was not seduced by the most dangerous of all
idolators of the state and enemies of individualism, not seduced
that is, by Hegel.

For, after all, it was Hegel who ended his review of Schiller's
Wallenstein with the words: "Ghastly, incredible! Death wins
over life! This isn't tragic but horrible!" — How optimisticallty
rigid is this idealistic concept of drama which Hegel maintains
torturously because he is able to disregard everyone who has
namelessly gone up in smoke in the name of the "world spirit."

Burckhardt, at the age of twenty-four, was the first to admit,
and this ten years after Hegel's death, that the "historical conflicts of the warring world powers are the unresolvable ones,
which it remains to be seen who will win, before one knows who
is right." Only Goethe had just as sober a concept of history as

Burckhardt, especially after his study of its absolutely incon-
solable Bohemian version; but Goethe never uttered his view in
public.

Burckhardt is singularly valiant in the way in which he throws
out of the theater all its classical laws, because he — unlike the
triumvirate Lessing, Goethe, and Schiller — already knows that
the "full, infinite source of individualism, to which the merely
moral dramatist remains impervious, and its ethical opposites"
only reveals itself to the one who admits to himself that history
"by and large does not know good and evil, but only this way or
that way."

As a student in Berlin during the Biedermeier period, Burckhardt already sees something which, a full hundred years later,
the then Nestor of the Berlin science of history, Friedrich Mei-
neke, failed to appreciate; and failed to do so despite his correspondence with the Göttingen historian Kaehler, who himself
was sufficiently deidealized by the battles of encirclement of
World War II to acknowledge again that "fate" is also a factor
in history.

When Burckhardt stated that Thucydides might contain a fact
of the first order whose significance might not be appreciated
for hundreds of years, it was unlikely that he was so vain as to
think that he, too, is one of those authors "whose thousandfold
exploited books must be read anew by everyone, because they
show each reader and each century a new face and also to every
person at his or her stage in life." Perhaps it required the apoc-
alyptic regrouping which Hitler's war produced in Europe to
reopen our eyes to the fact that the stoic and anticontempora-
neous concept of history of the Berlin student of the pre–1848
revolutionary period also preformulated the style of the new
drama, which is still binding for us today. This style creates
pieces which, though they "do not intentionally ignore the eter-
nal laws of morality," contain a higher and more poetic and

richer kind of law; and that law is a view of history without illusions. By changing from the ethical idealistic direction to the real and fatalistic direction, in the true historical sense of that word, one creates pieces where the "ethical conflicts" are side issues, and the main issue becomes that of representing individuals who are bound on the wheel of history and who in the age of universal conscription seek to intervene with their free will only in the rarest of cases, and then, generally speaking, only to be torn to bits by history's destructive machinery.

It is absolutely logical that Walter Muschg should have used his address on the occasion of Schiller's two hundredth birthday to demonstrate that in today's "war between freedom and barbarism" it has become impossible to maintain that *William Tell* is festive in any sense of the word; but that it is a tragedy and that it is drama as an act of lamentation.

Muschg said that in Basel without knowing that in the same city, twenty-one years before, on October 20, 1938, a modern Tell had bought a pistol in the weapons store of gunsmith Bürgin, Am Steinentor 13. And this modern Tell, a Swiss confederate by the name of Maurice Bavaud — his cousin is in the auditorium with us today — was beheaded on May 14, 1941, in Berlin.[6] Therefore, allow me to pronounce the first commemorative words on Swiss soil for this heroic and solitary figure whom you, the Swiss, brought forth, and to whom one can apply the ghastly aphorism of the Pole Stanislav Lec: "True martyrs are those whom one even denies that title."

Which is why you, Herr Regierungspräsident, ladies and gentlemen, will agree with me when I say that whoever lives and celebrates and who lets himself be celebrated should — if only fleetingly — recall one of those who did not enjoy the opportunity to live, to celebrate and to be celebrated.

On All Souls Day, after vainly looking for them for weeks, I finally visited the eighty-six-year-old parents and the sister of

Maurice Bavaud who live in Boudry, a village near Neuchâtel. I also saw the house he was born in, seventy meters away from the three marvelous old city fountains in Neuchâtel . . . no one has come more idyllically into this world, grown up more cared for than in this mailman's family with five children. Beloved, talented as a painter already at age twelve, tall, beautiful as a young warrior Homer might have depicted — although his uncle, a theologian, always called him "pacifist" instead of by his first name — Maurice becomes a mechanic because that's what his father wants, but then reads a book about missionaries in the Congo and goes to a seminary in France to study for the priesthood. His sister recalls that "he was always looking for an ideal."

We who are presently stupefied by the good luck of peace are then easily tempted to accuse such a sagalike figure — who sets out at age twenty-two to kill the man who one year later touched off the avalanche of war which killed fifty-six million people — of a lack of realism. That is unjustified! For precisely this, at precisely this time, was what the former head of the British Artillery (who was subsequently promoted during the war to brigadier general and governor of Gibraltar) and then military attaché to Berlin,[7] Sir Noel Mason-MacFarlane, was planning too. Sir Noel proves that the origin of a shot into the chest of the most horrendous figure of recorded history (during one of the cacophonous "Führer birthday parades" — Mason-MacFarlane's apartment, Sophienestrasse 1, was opposite the grandstand) could never be reconstructed. But this Scotsman, who unlike the Swiss assassin perhaps needed to hire a sharpshooter, could not discuss this decision alone with his conscience, the only authority which should have prohibited him from committing the deed, but instead with Downing Street.

The two German assassins, Elser and Stauffenberg, whose bombs at least tore a few Nazis out of the "calm eye of the hurricane," as Felix Hartlaub called Hitler's circle, both had excellent opportunities to escape unrecognized But this fellow from Neuchâtel did not. When he set out after a carefree vacation with his family and changed his francs in Basel to 555 marks, he knew with absolute certainty that he was setting off toward his own destruction.

In fact, he was more realistic than the two bomb setters, because when Stauffenberg's bomb, although it exploded right under Hitler's table, failed to tear the dictator apart, Field Marshal Rommel, who then had to take poison, said: "Wasn't there a captain with an army pistol?"[8] No, there was no German with a pistol, there was only this Swiss confederate! And he was there six years sooner than the detonator of the German General staff. . . .

And Hitler himself regarded this Catholic theology student (who "kept failing to get his shot off, and only by accident") as even more dangerous than the carpenter Johann Georg Elser. As Hitler's table partner noted: "The testimony of this Swiss was always of particular interest to him [Hitler] inasmuch as it confirmed him in his belief that there is no stopping an idealistic-minded assassin who is willing to sacrifice his life for his plan. He therefore understood perfectly why 90 percent of the assassinations attempted in the course of history had succeeded."[9] Hitler felt that the Swiss confederate belonged to the rarest category of assassins, to the idealists. "However, the number of idealistic assassins who were dangerous to him had always been small. The bourgeoisie and the Marxists numbered scarcely any assassins among them who were willing to give their lives. Therefore the only ones who posed a danger to him were those who had been incited by the Catholic priests in their confessional chambers, or nationalistically minded persons in the countries occupied by our troops." The tyrant expressed himself in this and a similar vein several times about Bavaud.

This is not the moment to fill you in on the details of a biography which Plutarch would have to recount, and which at some point will find a chronicler of that rank. (Until now only two historians, Hoffman from Montreal and Oldenhage from Koblenz, have followed the tracks of this Swiss, tracks which had already become nearly invisible despite the fact that Hitler mentioned Bavaud several times — and would have remained concealed if the Englishman David Irving had not secured them: he also found the man who had taken down a Hitler monologue on September 6, 1941. Since Hitler had no guest for lunch that day, the tyrant spoke nearly unadornedly about "the Swiss waiter" — Bavaud was never a waiter — and "recounted by what good fortune he had escaped his certain death.")

If one inspects the Maurice Bavaud dossier in the Bern archives (which are not even complete any longer because of secret incursions)[10] we, as Germans, are confronted by the accusatory question which Gerhart Hauptmann already raised in 1928, ten years before Bavaud set out, in his homage to *William Tell*: "Why can't we consider this work in every respect our own? Why did God want it that according to its name and place of action and its most intensive radiance it had to be left to the Swiss? Would it not be the annual festival of a free and inwardly self-confident Germany if it had the German people as its hero?"

No, it was our fate as Germans not to produce the Tell of the year 1938 (though at least Johann Georg Elser stepped forth at the same time and did so from *our* midst); it was left to us to produce only the executioners of this truly altruistic confederate! How every slip of paper in the Bern dossier seizes the heart of the observer! Or the letters — in the hands of his siblings — or the so-called Führer-informations about the interrogations, and the executioners' cant in the file-filled dungeons in Koblenz and Paris. Or the few photos which the parents own, such as that of the five-year-old with his little sister and his mother and the father in his postman's uniform, or also the highly impressive portrait of the vigorous twenty-one-year-old idealist, of September 1937! Out of what profound psychic distress were these letters written; yes, occasionally as though his heart were giving out: the letters of the searching, fearing, misled, then finally knowing — and knowing *what*! — father. In happier times, the sister now tells us, the father had occasionally quarreled with Maurice, but not seriously, because he had sung the "Internationale" at home. I will never forget the completely altered, suddenly nervous, previously so self-assured handwriting of the shocked man from Neuchâtel, rue du Seyon 3a, on June 10, 1940, when, after the judicial bandits from Berlin have already surpressed six letters from Maurice (the prisoner was not allowed to write a single political word) the father is finally informed, by mail, that his son is condemned to the guillotine, but has no idea why; or whether Maurice is still alive! How the father is so "composed" after receiving this news that in his letter to the government in Bern he mistakes — literally in a "stupor" — the month in which he is writing.

A commemorative word should also be pronounced for Dr. Franz Wallau, Bavaud's court-appointed Berlin attorney, whose deadly courageous attempts to save Bavaud at least from the guillotine "produces the greatest astonishment" in the Führer's Chancellory as well as among the individual members of the Senate which pronounced the death sentence. The "acting president" of the "People's Court" thus denounces the valiant lawyer on January 5, 1940, at the so-called National Socialist Association of the Keepers of Justice, which promptly excludes Wallau from this professional organization. Yet Wallau — it is a miracle — survived despite the fact that Reichsleiter Martin Bormann demanded, in writing, that he be punished!

So there were gaps in the net of pursuit and defense! For example it was incomprehensible to the court how Bavaud, a foreigner, and as the only one, could have succeeded in obtaining a seat on the honorary grandstand at the Munich procession on November 9, and even in the first row! Or to have penetrated into the Führer's own residence in Munich, the *Braune Haus*, and to speak there not just with the guards but with adjudants, high-placed legal officials, who even recommended that he go to the Führer's Chancellory in Berlin, which he then tried to do, only to be told that the Chancellory had followed its master into the vicinity of Berchtesgaden. Bavaud risked this too. He, who had been the most peaceful of men at home and had to learn to shoot a pistol only now, rents a boat on Lake Ammensee and takes potshots at little paper ships which he sets out on the water from his skiff! Yes, he even held target practice in the woods surrounding Hitler's mountain retreat, the Berghof!

It is also awe-inspiring how Bavaud, for weeks on end, endures the pressure of his solitary enterprise. Muschg emphasized the masterfulness of Schiller's concept when he refused to let Tell participate in the Rürtli Oath and left him as a loner, and with "this much-criticized feature lent the folk drama a twist which we perceive as brilliant today, now that the relationship between the individual and the state has also become problematic again in democracy."

The spiritual exhaustion following the attempted assassination allowed the Munich assassin Elser (who had gone his solitary way for months with instinctive certainty) to walk like a sleepwalker into the arms of two harmless customs officials. The same weariness evidently also made Bavaud forget to destroy the envelope addressed to Hitler, an envelope which was *empty*, and which for that reason alone produced the torture of the interrogations. The pistol found on Bavaud would never have sufficed to convict him. How one berates fate — whatever that is — once one knows that the great man was detected by a railway conductor only because he lacked the proper ticket! Maurice set out on his last attempt to assassinate Hitler with only five marks left in his pocket. He set out on foot, walked at night, to save these last five marks, and tried to reach the branch of the Reich Chancellory which had traveled with Hitler into the mountains. Then he decides to turn around, grabs a bit to eat, and buys a ticket as far as Freilassing, so as to sneak — all he has left now is one mark and 52 pfennigs — into the train to Paris. And only because he is a foreigner, for no other reason, do the Augsburg police hand him over to the Gestapo.

All these details are material for that process of assimilation which the future will initiate. I mean the process of how "the imagination of many people will continue to build on such a figure all by itself," the process which Burckhardt regards as the significant criterion "so that greatness becomes possible." The fragment of his lecture *Murder as a Remedy* sets out from the position that "in the absence of all legal means . . . [the individual] becomes the judge of his own cause." According to Burckhardt, historical greatness therefore only very rarely remains an undiscussed fact, is only very rarely taken for granted without being discussed, as for example with Caesar or with Mao today. Generally, greatness is a time-consuming, oft-interrupted growing process, at first a much-discussed process of accretion. I don't know of anyone living today of whom I am as convinced as I am of Bavaud that even in the remote future "the imagination of many people will continue to build on such a figure all by itself." After all, it is the historically unique satanism of the originator of Auschwitz that makes these singular opponents so valuable for humanity: the very few who sought to spare the totality — the allies — the horrible blood sacrifices which it took to kill the fellow from Braunau.

Only this still: no one took a more lonely walk to the guillotine, consoled not even by the priest (whose unsurpassingly nauseating Nazi letter to father Bavaud ends with the assurance that

Bavaud had brought "shame" on his parents!). Maurice went to the guillotine after twenty-eight months of prison. For seventeen months he had waited each day for that horse butcher Röttger who — together with others — hanged and beheaded in Plötz-ensee Prison in Berlin. Although visits by members of the Swiss embassy in Berlin were not unprecedented (occasionally they could also send trial observers), Herr Frölicher, Bern's ambassador to Hitler, never sent a compatriot to visit Bavaud, and then justified this ommission on April 2, 1940, a day on which Bavaud was still alive, by pointing out to his superiors "the despicable intentions of the condemned man."

When Maurice's cell was unlocked thirteen months later, at 8 P.M. on May 12, 1941, so that he could be told that he would be beheaded at dawn the next day, he was reading Descartes. "My blood has stayed cool and it will stay that way until six o'clock, the moment when my head falls off," goes the second sentence of his farewell letter, which is written in a firm hand and which I found at his sister's house because the parents to this day cannot bear keeping it at theirs. Cold blood (still to be able to say that!) and a well-honed intelligence also characterized his ceaseless efforts to get off a shot. The People's Court judged that twice, on November 9 and 12, Bavaud had acutely endangered the Führer's life, and Hitler himself was never again to rest easy because of this "Swiss sniper," as he called him. Even years later, he said that because of assassins like this Swiss "waiter" (for he did not dare admit even to his closest circle that a student, a theologian at that, had brought himself to the point of wanting to murder him) one could never again march through such narrow streets as those in Munich! Hitler feared Bavaud as a model, and keeping the attempt a secret was ordered specifically because "dissemination of this news . . . might be suited to bring similar plans to fruition."

Please note how, so typically of the time, "individual" is used deprecatingly as a reprimand! Johann Georg Elser, who watched the same procession of Nazi bigwigs in Munich that Bavaud did, and did so in order to make studies for the assassination attempt at the Bürgerbräukeller a year later, was a worker and artisan, a brilliant carpenter, an autodidact who had learned to rig up clocks and bombs. Hitler prohibited any of that from ever becoming known! According to the newspapers, Elser was merely a "subject" — and this too then is part of the hatred of our time of the loner: that no one believed that Elser *could* have acted by himself. The public was kept in the dark about the fact that he had acted entirely by himself even when the Gestapo had long since abandoned all doubts on that score; for, after Hitler's minions had tortured Elser into a clump of blood so that he would scream out the names of his "accomplices,"[12] one of the torturers came on the idea of forcing the victim to rebuild the bomb in prison. Lo and behold, the re-creation became such a showpiece that it was shown to every rookie Nazi cop to drive the fear of God into him! Yet in public the assassin was deprived of the honorary designation "lone wolf"; lies were spread that Elser was a "tool of the British Secret Service."

The real reason why the state mistrusts literature may be because literature insists on the freedom of choice; or rather, the individual's duty to choose. Schnitzler noted during the first of the World Wars that it is "the artful trick of politics to disregard the individual, to reckon in terms of masses, in contrast to the artist who dissolves the masses into individuals."[13] In fact, every piece of literature is an endorsement of the individual, and is that much more convincing the less the institutions allow the individual to be effective by himself and as a representational figure. Whereas "being human" would be a true virtue, "being realistic" is advertised as such today. As Ingmar Bergman said recently,[14] "Society is ultimately not a collective abstraction, it consists of individual human beings." And matters must be in a sorry state indeed if one actually needs to remind people of this because "the demand of the powers that be becomes more compelling than that of persons and their uniqueness. . . . This in fact explains why the preference for balladlike qualities is diminishing. . . ." (Ernst Jünger)[15]

It is only too logical that our society then sics psychiatrists on the heroes of ballads when one of them finally reappears to shove the helmsman of an entire age overboard for the sake of an entire generation! Just as in 1939 the Nazis sicced Bumke, their most famous psychiatrist, on Elser, so they put two psychiatrists on Bavaud in the hope that they would declare this "individual" to be mentally defective! Even doctors working in conjunction with legal experts were incapable of accomplishing that feat of deception. After misleading his interrogators for months on end, the Swiss confederate told the People's Court on December 18, 1939, that he "conceived the criminal plan to kill the German Führer entirely on his own. . . . He regards the Führer and Chancellor a danger to humanity, primarily also to Switzerland whose independence he threatens. However, he has been brought to this decision primarily by religious considerations. He felt he was doing a service to mankind and to all Christendom with his act because he felt that the Catholic organizations and churches were being surpressed. . . . And the only reason he gave up his undertaking in Bischofswiesen on November 12, 1938, was because he had run out of money. Otherwise he would have continued to wait for an opportune moment for the execution of his murderous plan."

And then right after Bavaud's corpse had presumably been taken to the anatomical section, Hitler provided this Swiss, who always exemplified danger, the only distinction which he could actually lend him: he did not make Bavaud merely into one among uncounted other martyrs; no, he raised him high above the figures of the history of the time and entwined him in mythology by placing him directly next to William Tell. Hitler prohibited the play by the same name on June 3, 1941! And this was followed a year later, on December 12, by Hitler's edict that even the "pithy sayings and songs" from the now prohibited drama (which could no longer be taught as a text in schools, or lent out by libraries) would have to disappear from all new textbooks.[17]

Herr Regierungspräsident, ladies and gentlemen, I — a German — wanted with this report about your tragic confederate, the tragic Tell who armed himself in 1938 in Basel to liberate Europe and my fatherland from Hitler, I wanted to give over to all the Swiss people the great gratitude that I feel for this prize, for this city of Basel.

II

THE NOTES

1. In Olten, on the occasion of a guest performance by the Basel City Theater, on October 29, 1963; some people, however, claim that the Olten police prevented the demonstrators from storming the theater during the performance.

Two press notices from Olten, of October 30, 1963. First from *Der Neue Morgen*:

A Deserved Trouncing

In Olten the audience expressed its disapproval and outrage at the performance of the gruesome, tendentious German play *The Deputy* in appropriate if at times perhaps too vehement a fashion. The demonstration in the theater itself was perfectly fine. However, those people who invoke the phrase "law and order" seem to think that it permits only *them* to express their opinion, but not those who are *against* what is shown and performed. It was instructive to observe who opposed the manifestions of disapproval. More likely than not these were some of the Freemasons and anticlerical groups from Olten, as well as the miserable pseudointellectual sediment, and also a few morally rather questionable figures. These people are unimportant and showed who they really are at the end of the performance, with their heavy applause and with the exclamation: "Out with the Catholic!" What remains noticeable is the intransigence of certain representatives of the authorities. We were gravely disappointed by people who we assumed until today would be loyal, and we will not forget this at the next elections. *These* people, too, were intent on being provocative and on keeping anti-Catholic sentiments alive, even on exacerbating them. This provocation was arranged and its purpose was achieved insofar as the Catholic population, not only of Olten but also of its surrounding region, felt called upon to demonstrate and to point the finger at the provocateurs.

Some behavior by the officials bears police-state features. Yet the police themselves behaved correctly toward both sides. Still, it was questionable why catcallers and particularly vociferous whistlers were bounced while shameless shouters on the other side, among them a few Olten industrialists and lawyers, who were beside themselves with injured dignity, were left untouched. What the *Securitas* then performed with their nightsticks was undignified. Do the two police forces need to employ such people to keep order?

The demonstration in front of the theater was a spontaneous action of primarily youthful groups. The people responsible for this are those circles who kindled the fire, namely the Theater Commission of Olten, which has made a thorough fool of itself and has lost all political and moral credibility.

If this commission, with its president in front, is tempted to engage a repeat performance of the piece, then one can obviously expect similar and even sharper defensive measures. That would also be the time to take a somewhat closer look at the ideology and motives of this commission.

All this has certain immediate consequences for the Catholic circles in Olten. The Olten theater has been discredited for a long time to come, it has turned out to be an incubator of interdenominational strife. Such a theater no longer deserves the support of public funds.

Everything that is reprimanded, lowered and pilloried here today could easily have been avoided . . . if one had canceled the performance of Hochhuth's *The Deputy* in Olten. It is as if one had absolutely wanted to produce a situation where one could then proclaim: "Lord, we thank you that we are not like these here!" . . .

The same day the *AZ* (Arbeiterzeitung) *Das Volk* wrote:

The Deputy with Ugly Noises

The people of Olten will long remember yesterday evening. For hours on end a whistling and howling horde of youths filled the main streets to demonstrate against the performance of Hochhuth's *The Deputy*. A large complement of security forces — police and *Securitas*— at times was scarcely able to keep the demonstrators in check.

Masses of demonstrators had been provided with tickets so as to sabotage the performance, and were equipped with whistles and other noisemaking instruments. There were stretches when the performance was drowned out by the deafening uproar. The police acted only very timidly, the troublemakers were able to employ their instruments unmolested even while the theater was brightly lit. One of the demonstrators even brought a trumpet along.

The actors performed their work with an admirable show of cool — during the pauses the applause for their achievement mingled with a cacophony of whistling, producing a veritable unending inferno.

When it became quiet in the theater the audience was treated to realistic background noise: The howling of the instigated youths penetrated the walls of the City Theater. They tried to overwhelm the guards at the doors, there were scuffles and the guards had to use their rubber truncheons.

There were also fights at the back of the theater where a few youths tried to barge in by breaking two panes of the stage door and throwing "stinkbombs" under it. They also stole the prop cart and pulled it out onto the street, where they slashed its tires.

But in general, the police remained in control of the situation. At the end of the performance the demonstrators on the street greeted the departing audience with boos. Choruses formed, shouting: "Begone with the Nazis." The police were only barely able to keep the through street to Hauenstein open. But the curious who had assembled behind the demonstrators were left generally unmolested.

Police estimated the crowd in the streets at three thousand, the majority of whom of course consisted of amused nonparticipants. The demonstrators were exclusively youths between the ages of fourteen and twenty who had been summoned from the surrounding communities, from Oensinger as far as Erlinsbach.

The official Catholic authorities had distanced themselves from the affair. However, leaflets calling for participation in the demonstration had been distributed in the churches the previous Sunday. The Catholic priest of Olten (St. Marien) found approximately 1000 such invitations on the stairs of his parsonage, which he was apparently meant to distribute. But since the leaflets had no signature and did not betray their origin in any other way, he refused to do so. It is said that the demonstration was organized by a wealthy private source.

After eleven P.M. the crowd dispersed and the streets became quiet. Those who understand these matters attribute the end of the demonstration to the fact that at eleven the last trains and buses leave for the Olten suburbs.

The loud screaming on the street of course made any sensible discussion of the piece itself impossible. Dr. P. Hagmann, the president of the Theater Commission, made the following comments in this regard:

"Considering the circumstances, the performance can only be called very good. After some initial nervousness the actors retained an admirable composure. There is no need for me to mention the behavior of the demonstrators."

In fact, this orchestrated whistle concert was more than embarrassing. Gray-haired men and snotnosed youths unabashedly held whistles in their mouths and showed that a good education had been wasted on them. The reluctant use of the forces of law and order was considered ridiculous by the audience which, incidentally, applauded several times. It was said that a more energetic showing could have restored order without any difficulty whatsoever.

It also became evident that the youths who had been urged to participate in the demonstration had not been very well informed. One fellow, asked to explain why he hollered "Begone with the Nazis," replied: "Anyone who is for *The Deputy* is for Hitler," which of course explains the eagerness with which the young team went into action.

Under these circumstances we are only too glad to hear that the official Catholic authorities distanced themselves from this affair. After having seen the performance we well understand how a Catholic might feel injured by the symbols that were shown. But we don't understand why it was necessary to react to them in that well-known style with mass howling and incited youths. Whoever had the idea of doing things this way — the course he took this time led entirely in the wrong direction.

The *Basler Volksblatt* hung out placards on December 16, 1976: "*Time Bomb from Hochhuth.*" This was supposed to call attention to the report in the newspaper about the synodic conference

of the Roman Catholic Church of the Canton of the City of Basel
in the main hall in Basel on December 15, 1976. The *Volksblatt*
wrote:

Giving the 1976 Basel art prize to Rolf Hochhuth has triggered
a delayed reaction: The synod conference of the RCC therefore
asked for an explanation and the church council sent a letter of
"astonishment" to the government. . . .

The synodal member Hans Baur resorted to the method of
claiming infraction against the synod. The Catholic side had
made an attempt to forget the injustice, but old wounds had
been ripped open again, many groups feel injured. A citizen of
this city could not understand, could not endorse such approval
of the judging and condemning of a pope by such a provocateur
and by a government counselor. Deacon Cavelti confirmed in
his letter of reply noticeable excitement among Catholics in
Basel. The boards of different organizations objected to this af-
frontery, which is why he called upon Government Counsel
Schneider, who expressed surprise at such an unintended reaction now that some years had passed since the performance.
The prize had artistic, not political, value. Besides, the Government Council as a whole did not unanimously agree to the
recommendation of the "jury."

The Church Council confirmed this conversation in a letter to
the government and expressed its astonishment.

The interpellant and his respondent are employing a calm
tone of voice. The plenary session remained quiet.

2. In the Munich *Abendzeitung* of May 10, 1963, was Dehler's reply to Foreign Minister Schröder's explanation of May 3,
1963 — "The federal government is deeply regretful" — for the
"minor inquiry of the delegates Majonica, Lemmer and com-

rades" in the *Bundestag* in Bonn. Reprinted in Fritz J. Raddatz (editor): *Summa iniuria oder Durfte der Papst schweigen? Hochhuth's Der Stellvertret in der öffentlichen Kritik* [Summa Inuira, or Should the Pope Have Remained Silent? Hochhuth's *The Deputy* and Its Public Criticism] (rororo aktuell 591, Reinbek, September 1963).

3. Reinhild Buhne: *Jeremias Gotthelf und das Problem der Armut* [Jeremias Gotthelf and the Problem of Poverty] (Bern: Francke Verlag, 1968).

4. *Der Zauber der Abstraktion* [The Magic of Abstraction], in *Euphorion* 58 (1964), then in *Neue Studien zur Tragischen Literaturgeschichte* [New Studies about the History of Tragic Literature] (Bern: Francke Verlag, 1965).

Muschg took four copies of the paperback to the aforementioned post office, pushed them toward the official — and keeled over dead. The recipients received the book together with the news that its author had died. Muschg still had the opportunity to hand me this essay collection personally, during my last visit. We talked about death because I was working on my "Everyman" — the framework for my tragedy *Soldiers* — without knowing how I would have death appear on stage. The Salzburg example was out of the question. We considered and dismissed various possibilities. Then Muschg told me about a visit, the first in years, which he had paid to Jaspers. Jaspers had told me that Muschg had spoken in a tone of hopelessness about contemporary German literature, there were no more great poets. . . .

Then, because of the state of helplessness that my formal problems had created in me, we again talked about death. Muschg finally ended it, saying: "Let's stop this, this is quite awful in Basel. They still have an ordinance left over from the time of the plague according to which a dead person has to be removed from his house the very same day, he can't even stay in the house overnight!" (Frau Muschg was not present. But a few days later she saw to it that her dead husband, who had been taken from the post office to the morgue, was transferred once more to their home, where I saw him lie in state around noon.) Muschg had suggested to me that I should not confront my bomber pilot with a figure of death but that the pilot should approach death within a *monologue interieur*. I had to stick to my opinion that drama, as distinct from the novel, could not do without a physical representation of death. And I finally solved my problem with the help of the photo of the incinerated woman from Dresden, the skeleton with the hairs which is reproduced in performances of *Soldiers* and in its published version. A few minutes before his last seminar, Muschg handed me a note once more recommending the *monologue interieur*. Since he died three days later, these may have been the last literary lines that he wrote: "Death as the unconscious 'other I' can also speak in such a way that his words can be grasped as the *monologue interieur* of the one whom he frightens. Death, then, can say something like: You don't need to be frightened of death. No hell awaits you, no limbo, but unfortunately no paradise either. No one is afraid of death any more today. People are only afraid to die; for, whoever dies cannot lie to himself, he knows the truth and sees his guilt which won't let him die in peace. That is why you are afraid of me. But I can console you: if you recognize your guilt, your life will not have been without meaning. Your fear of death is your fear of meaninglessness. I will liberate you from this dread if you admit that you are guilty."

5. Adorno: *Zur Dialektik des Engagement* [On the Dialectics of Commitment] (Berlin: Neue Rundschau, 1962): ". . . it con-

cerns highly concrete historical matters: the abnegation of the subject. . . ."

Adorno assumed precisely the same position as the vulgar Marxists according to whom it is not the individual but social forces and "conditions" that dominate historical processes. The communist Kurt Tuchoslky revised his own convictions in this matter from his own experience with "history." Two years before he committed suicide, having already immigrated to Sweden, he wrote the Zurich doctor Hedwig Müller on December 10, 1933: "You are right: people do not change. That is why I believe that Marx has created infinitely more harm than good with his teachings. His disciples are so arrogant, they have everything in writing, and of course that is bullshit: neither "men make history" nor does the milieu make men; both things occur through the interaction. It is amusing to note how people in the little sheet (*Weltbühne*) are infinitely slowly slipping away from the teachings in which they believed ever so firmly for so many years; they aren't aware of it themselves. Such a lack of psychology, of the simplest understanding of people, is fatal." (*Briefe aus dem Schweigen* [Reinbek: Rowohlt Verlag, 1977]).

In the above-mentioned essay Adorno also stated that "every commitment to the world must be broken so that the idea of a committed work of art can be maintained. . . . Literature which is committed, and literature which, as the ethical philistines want it, is there for mankind, betrays mankind by betraying the matter which might help mankind if only it did not behave as though it were helping."

To the best of my knowledge Peter Rühmkorf (in his contribution to a Festschrift on the occasion of Adorno's sixtieth birthday) was the only one who dared take up that challenge. Contra dogma he declared how we had come by Adorno's esthetic, and what one could say against it: "Formalism, the art with nothing in mind but art, formalism and its whole theoretical system, fit so perfectly into the political scheme of the owners of society because, on the one hand, you could ring out the complete freedom of the individual, and on the other the danger that the creations of this freedom might bear witness against the free economy was automatically excluded. Because the bourgeois art critics ultimately really liked the owners of society and because none of them really wanted to have any changes (and those on the right of course even less than the few on the left) that is why the artistic laws also feel nicely into line. Art was called autonomous, timeless, unconditional, harmless. Three was no need for any disruptive elements in it. . . .

"When all one does is expect information about poetry and its possibilities, such considerations then may seem incommensurate with the 'pure subject'; and those who dislike politics in art as much as they hate bad breath will turn up their noses in disgust, and not even be entirely unjustified in doing so. For nothing seems more remote from the airy nature of the poem than effectiveness, influence, power and determination; and what seems entirely incommensurate with it are those minor upheavals of everyday politics. Names like Dufhues, for example, and Paczensky, Group 47 or the 'Spiegel' Affair — so one would think — obviate the possibility for stylization all by themselves. A verse that prides itself on its form would have to exclude that from the very beginning. This objection does not sound all that unjustified, yet it is just as deeply stuck in the ruling ideology of form as the view that art should have no opinion, as the view that the poem has no place in public, and as the thought that poetry must resign itself to impotence from the very beginning and as a matter of principle. For the moment let us be so naïve as to ask why poetry should, must, can, or could not do any of these things? Why should the contemporary poet as a matter of principle do without what poetry in many ages and countries always laid claim to: the right to become vigorously involved in the affairs of the everyday? What one should do first of all is allow poetry an unbiased position and the poet the fundmental right to perceive and take up what he considers important; and not immediately decree a code of behavior and a set of prohibitions whose seemingly golden rules turn out to be made of fool's gold already upon first inspection."

Adorno immediately became more reasonable, but not in public. In a letter to Rühmkorf of February 13, 1964, he wrote: ". . . You will believe me when I say that I am as uncomfortable with works that are made up solely of tapestry patterns as I am with the equivalent in music and painting, which are so easily prized among us. I only mean that one should say very precisely what one is against, and name the names which are odious." To be found in Rühmkorf's autobiography, *Die Jahre die Ihr Kennt* (Reinbek: Rowohlt Verlag, 1972).

6. Bavaud wrote his farewell letter to his parents and siblings on May 12, and expected to be beheaded the following morning. We hope that his prison-keepers — in Plötzensee, Königsdamm 6, Haus 3 — misinformed him; for Maurice was executed one morning later, on May 14, 1941. If he had heard of his imminent execution already on the twelfth, he would have had to wait two nights and one day with this certainty in mind. The brutality with which the executions were performed makes a postponement likely. We know that one participant in the 20th of July plot was led twice to the gallows; he was brought back the first time because he was still needed as a witness. . . . Most of the eyewitnesses of these executions are dead, and of those of who are alive only a few are willing to speak out. Yet Hans Halter, who is from Berlin, got some of these remaining witnesses to talk and reported about this in the August 1979 issue of *Der Spiegel*, of which we provide an excerpt that will convey some

of the gruesomeness of the last moments, including Bavaud's:

"The severed head, eyes wide open, fell into a wicker basket. Because the body of the condemned man was not firmly fastened to the scaffold, it was able to shake itself free at the last moment. The torso reared up, the legs raised, and the clogs were shaken off.

"The blood spurted in a high arc from the torso into the gully. . . . The state presented itself in all its might and magnificence to whoever was transferred from life to death here: the hangman in his cutaway, his three assistants in black suits; the judge in his red robe, the state's attorney and the priest in black robes; the Department of Justice official in hunting-green cloth; the institute doctor in white jacket, the guests in uniform. A crucifix on the table, two tall candelabras on the wall."

No concentration camp guard was at work here, with sadistic inclinations or perhaps drunk. Law and order ruled at this place of death; each step was determined by a regulation. There were tickets for the guests and a sign saying: "The German greeting is out of place here." The officials expected the victim to be "calm and composed" and to behave according to protocol. Only rarely did one of them fail to live up to that role.

"I can't recall a single one who cried, screamed or defended himself," the Protestant pastor Hermann Schrader, eighty, who witnessed dozens of executions, told me. "It also calmed some of them down when I told them that I would stand behind them until the knife fell." That never took long. Only seconds — twenty to twenty-five in peacetime, during the war only seven or even four — passed from the command "Executioner, do your duty!" to the report "State Attorney, the verdict has been discharged." An official noted down the time on a DIN A 5 form which has been kept to this day. . . .

Of the approximately three thousand who were forced to die in this quadrangle, often not even a photo exists. The oldest, a worker, was eighty-three; the youngest barely seventeen. Forty-one couples died in Berlin Plötzensee who were unable to take leave of each other. Mothers who had given birth in prison were not spared. Justice went before mercy. Two hundred and fifty women were beheaded. An old shoemaker cut off their hair on their last evening, so as to lay the neck bare. A prison priest recalls: "The haircut was a perquisite for the shoemaker. He did it with equanimity, without being moved and with a certain dull satisfaction."

Only few officials took actual pleasure in the killings. One exception was the medical orderly of House III who is still remembered by Viktor von Gostomski, now a publisher in Weiden/Oberpfalz. This orderly gave no medication to those who were about to be executed, and often more than three hundred people were in Plötzensee at any one time. The orderly said: "You're gonna lose your noggin anyway." The prison guards who had to escort the victims from their cells to the place of execution received eight cigarettes per head as a reward. Herr von Gostomski recalls that he once heard two guards quarrel, with one accusing the other of having been pushy in performing his duty so as to get more cigarettes.

The officials of the National Socialist Department of Justice of course had to help out occasionally when a young prisoner became panicky, and stuff a towel down a screaming candidate's mouth. They were not reprimanded for this. Most of them kept their jobs after the war.

. . . The newspaper delivery woman Emmi Zehden from Berlin-Gatow died because she belonged to Jehovah's Witnesses, thereby allegedly decimating the people's will to defend itself. William Otto Bauer, a traveling salesman for a refrigerator company, became a victim of the knife because in 1942 he had accurately guessed that there were two possibilities: either Hitler kills us or we kill Hitler. Officially he "lost his honor forever"

— like that mail carrier who stole six cigarettes from an army package and lost his head for it.

The entire "civilian" justice system was working toward the death house, not only Freisler's People's Court as the keepers of justice like to claim today. No judge, not a one, has been brought to justice for that so far. All of them get their pensions.

Why should the executioner, of all people, have to atone? Did he commit a greater crime? "Well, you know, Herr Röttger, that was a big strong man," says his neighbor, who is eighty-four now. "Always nicely dressed. A Justice Department official he is, he told me. That's a large concept, very elastic." Right you are, Mother Bonczek. . . .

Justice alone takes a different view of this. In a friendly conversation the present head of the penal institution Plötzensee, a gentle melancholic, emphasizes that Röttger really was not an official — he did his work for an annual fee of 3000 Reichsmarks plus a premium of 30 marks per head.

Thus on the seventh night of September 1943, to "reduce the number of condemned as quickly as the directives demanded," he earned a total of 5580 RM, for 186 executions, four of which were performed "by accident" — it all went so quickly that the inspector lost the overview and had four prisoners led to the place of execution by mistake. No proceedings were instituted against the inspector; however, he was "seriously reprimanded."

The last meal before the execution had long since been eliminated at this time. No death bells tolled, and Röttger's assistants — the brothers Thomas, one of them a smithy, the other the innkeeper of the tavern Sängerklause — always tossed two corpses into one coffin. Because a person without a head needs less room, the boxes were twenty centimeters shorter than usual, and covered with sawdust to absorb the blood.

The German postwar attitude to those who opposed Hitler (not on the external but on the internal front) and who usually came to a horrible end, becomes especially clear when one compares the small pensions which some — but by no means all — relatives of the victims of Hitler justice receive to the undiminished high pensions paid to the Justice murderers in the Federal Republic, none of whom ever had to appear before a court of law as long as he had only studied law. This attitude is drastically clarified by a report of the Englishman Sefton Delmer, whose memoirs retained what he was forced to discover even fifteen months after Hitler's suicide in the cellar of the Charité in Berlin:

"It was in the basement of the Berliner Charité that I found my first clearcut example of that peculiar dualism prevalent in post-Hitler Germany — the ambivalent attitude held by today's Germans toward those who fought against Hitler for a better world and a better Germany. The men who rule Germany today often like to use these resistance fighters as an alibi for their nation, as a defense against the accusation of collective guilt. However, as soon as they feel themselves to be in a strong enough position, they will speak scornfully of these same men, branding them as traitors.

"In the sour-smelling gloom of the hospital's basement, two wooden tubs filled with brine stood against the whitewashed wall. The attendant took off their covers, one after the other, to show me what was inside. I stared in horror at a collection of human heads, which bobbed up and down like apples in a bucket of water as the attendant stirred them about.

"As the attendant explained to me, these were the heads of Hitler's opponents, who had been executed by decapitation in the terrible prison of Plötzensee. Many of these heads had once graced the shoulders of Germans, and others those of Norwegians, Frenchmen, or Poles. The old man explained further that it had been common practice in Plötzensee after executions for the heads to be sent to the Charité, so that the anatomy students

could dissect them and learn from them. However, because at
that time more heads were being delivered to the hospital than
could possibly be put to use, the remainder were placed in these
containers filled with brine. Yes, the attendant insisted, the students still use these heads, even though Hitler and Himmler
have long been dead and the Third Reich is but an ugly
memory.

"In fact, it was one year and three months after Hitler's suicide that Frankie Lynder and I made this chilling discovery. But
apart from the elderly attendant (a Social Democrat, whom
Frankie had telephoned from his office at the German Press
Service in order to ask him about these heads), no one else in
the Charité had found it shocking that students and professors
continued to conduct what was basically a typically National
Socialist policy of "utilization of the worthless" with the remains
of these men, who by rights should have been considered heroes
and martyrs and accorded every conceivable honor by the Germans as well as the Allies. Following reports by Frankie and
myself along with a lead article in the *Telegraf* written by the
editor-in-chief, Arno Scholz, the dissections finally ceased, and
the heads were given an honorable burial and placed to rest in
a communal grave."

It becomes evident from a so-called Führer-information — at
times these were printed, and in such large letters that Hitler
could read them without glasses — that the Reichsminister of
Justice kept Hitler au courant about the testimony in the Bavaud
trial. Bavaud's testimony on page 35 of the indictment therefore
will have made a particular impression on the dictator: ". . . he
[Bavaud] explained that by performing his actions he accepted
the possibility of any kind of punishment, and even counted on
being lynched by the outraged population if he had succeeded
in fulfilling his attempt on November 9, 1938."

Later, after the 20th of July assassination attempt had failed, Hitler joked about the fact that the conspiratorial officers had not shot him down when they — for example, the chief of communications at the Führer headquarters, General Feldgiebel — had the lightly wounded Hitler at their mercy only a few meters away, after the explosion which Stauffenberg had set off. (See David Irving: *Hitler and his Fieldmarshalls.*)

What now follows, with considerable misgivings, is the unabbreviated indictment and death sentence against Maurice Bavaud; and with such misgivings because on many, many pages Bavaud's executioners have the word, not Bavaud. And this situation constitutes the beginning of the injustice of all history writing, or at least its problematic nature. For Bavaud's executioners not only isolated him for an entire year and even prevented him from contacting his attorney during that period — that is, until he was actually indicted — but they also supressed at least six letters to his parents and did not permit him — like any other prisoner — to write a single political word: all this creates a displacement that borders on a falsification of history, yes, that *is* one. And although we consider our readers adults, it is still possible that some of them when they read the indictment might react as foolishly and impulsively and stupidly-cockily as the Zurich historian Urner does at the expense of the Nazi victim Bavaud. Because, since Bavaud left no political testament behind, Urner judges him almost exclusively by the picture his hangmen have drawn; that is, from this indictment and this death sentence! But the picture, which Hitler's beadles "sketch" and which Urner, lusting for documents and believing in documents, accepts at face value, resembles Maurice Bavaud about as much as a caricature of a Jew in Julius Streicher's *Stürmer* resembles a normal Jew. . . .

The fact that Urner apparently never got a single whiff of what it means to live under a dictatorship does not excuse his incomprehension of the language which even underlings of a dictator have to use. And how much more need to conceal himself had that man who was in the claws of Hitler's justice which intended to convict him of the most heinous of imaginable deeds: the intention of finishing off the tyrant!

And when we read the testimony from the Gestapo prison we must calculate not only Bavaud's intentional distortion; we — who have been spared by war and stupefied by peace — must also calculate the distortion that solitary confinement in the Nazi cellars must necessarily have produced in a foreigner without command of the German language, who was left heartlessly in the lurch also by his Swiss compatriots. In any event, Bavaud had been in an isolation cell for a year, isolated also from all counsel, when Herr Lautz (that Reich attorney general who is merrily consuming his pension in Lübeck today, despite the fact that he expressly demanded death by hanging for all of the officers of the 20th of July 1944 plot) wrote his indictment of Bavaud. Bavaud not only kept his *reason* until he was brought to the guillotine; that is, after twenty-eight months, seventeen of which he spent waiting every night and day for the executioner. Bavaud also kept his *decency*, as his farewell letter demonstrates; and that all by itself sufficed to provide him with the most magnificent human grade, inasmuch as we who have (so far) been spared by history can even be so presumptuous as to give out a grade to one who was "done in" by history; done in by history because he — and that is what one should mention in Bavaud's case — was, for example, the only human being, the *only* one, who took it upon himself to kill Hitler with a pistol; the only one who accepted his own death through lynch justice as part of the absolute certainty of the bargain. . . .

So as to be able to evaluate the insolence, the absurdity, of the "reprimands" Urner gives his compatriot, younger readers in particular need to be reminded of certain difficulties. For example, one of the highest-placed officials in Hitler Germany, the undersecretary of the Foreign Office, Weizsäcker, had to disguise himself constantly while speaking and writing so as to retain the possibility of being able to walk (from the Foreign Office) across to Hitler in the Reich Chancellory to talk him out of possible war plans at least for a few days! That is the same Weizsäcker who kept pointing out that all documents written under a tyranny provide insight into the psyche and the intentions of its author only if one reads between the lines, remembering *for whom* they were formulated; that is, not for *us*, the posteritity that was spared, but for those who replied to words of opposition invariably with the guillotine, and who were somehow to be influenced for the good or the better, however briefly.

Weizsäcker in his memoirs as well as in his secret journal often circled around the question whether he was even *allowed* to remain in office, or whether he should not step aside for his brother, Viktor von Weizsäcker, the psychiatrist and doctor of the mad in Heidelberg! ". . . if I didn't feel like a kind of director in Winnenden, I would have had to go fishing on Lake Constance long ago. What keeps me going is the thought that I have three sons who are of military age and a captain who will soon be a son-in-law. It probably would be better for my good name if I went angling for whitefish," Weizsäcker noted in his diary on July 3, 1938. That diary's editor comments: "Winnenden was the insane asylum in the vicinity of Stuttgart. . . . Two dashes at the end of a sentence mean that Weizsäcker means exactly the opposite." (Incidentally, Weizsäcker then did lose one son and his son-in-law during the war.)

It would also have been better for Bavaud's "good name" if like the rest of us he had done nothing at all. Then his compatriot Urner would not be chiding him as a "foolhardy dilettante" or "juvenile delinquent and occasional subscriber to an anti-

Semitic journal"! Herr Urner was none of those things, but was
always "good." Since Herr Urner never let himself say something in public about his tragic confederate but waited until I
exposed myself with the first report about Bavaud, he did not
become guilty of that "paradoxical distortion" of which he accuses my 1976 Basel speech where I call Bavaud Tell 38. This
speech demonstrated why Hitler forbade Schiller's drama immediately after he received the news of the execution of Bavaud
on June 3, 1941, but this is mentioned as little by Urner as is
the fact that until my speech no one in Switzerland had ever
said a word about Bavaud. . . .

On the other hand, the team of Swiss authors Niklaus Meienberg and Villi Hermann have begun to do research, and have
performed exemplary source work with results that are as exciting as they are depressing. Hermann and Meienberg and their
cameraman Hans Stürm went to the roots, to the witnesses. They
even went to the "barber" (who now lives under a different name)
who used to shave the men in Plötzensee before they were executed. That barber then had to wash the blood off the cut-off
heads and tar the torsos, so that the short boxes which served
as coffins would not cause any consternation because of blood
seeping out of them in crematoria, cemeteries, or morgues.
These two authors also took the trouble to visit the daughter of
Ambassador Frölicher, who had been in Berlin with her father,
and they found out that indeed there existed the possibility of
freeing Bavaud by exchanging him for Germans who were aton-
ing for political crimes in Swiss prisons. But Bern was as un-
interested in Bavaud as were Frölicher and his embassy people
in Berlin. (Frölicher doesn't even mention Bavaud in his diary,
which Meienberg read.) Meienberg and Hermann were also able
to correct me on one essential point: since Hitler himself apparently mistook Bavaud — whose name he never mentioned

— for a waiter or "Swiss waiter," whom he mentions occasionally, I believed that he intentionally gave him an undignified profession so as not to have to admit that a theology student or seminarian had wanted to kill him. This assumption may hold true for several statements by Hitler. He sometimes also mistakes the 1937 and 1938 assassination attempts as we know from his Table Talks, including the one reprinted here (noted down on September 6, 1941 by SA Standarten-Führer Dr. Werner Koeppen, Rosenberg's liaison man at Hitler's headquarters). But Meienberg and Hermann found out that a Swiss waiter, Ludwig Schmitt from Basel, was also beheaded, evidently after assassination attempts became known. . . . They report about it in their book.

Whoever takes the trouble to look up witnesses and even the hangmen at the places where the murders occurred certainly lacks Urner's academic limitations and inability to empathize with the conditions under which someone had to "live" who — however briefly — like Bavaud went into the German Reich to kill Hitler! Meienberg and Hermann possess what Urner lacks entirely: the imagination to represent Bavaud as the one and the *only* one of an entire age who dared to want to shoot Hitler from the front and as someone who spent twenty-eight horrendous months in Nazi prisons before being executed. As though I even had the possibility of idealizing such an ideal figure, a bearer of ideas of such a lonely rank, as Urner accuses me of doing! Meienberg writes:

"The motive for the assassination did not quite correspond to our dreams. . . . At first we wanted to react like the Swiss filmmaker Rolf L., who rejected the project with the words: 'I don't want to create a memorial for an anti-Semite.' But then came the thought that someone who had seriously planned to kill the lousy dog and who accepted being killed himself as part of the bargain should not be measured by our standards but rather by his own, and that we should not force this assailant into our mold."

That is how it is. Why should we, where do we get the right — after Auschwitz — to focus on peripheral, abstruse, incidental and stupid anti-Semitic sayings such as Maurice repeated as a student (no different from boys in England or Italy at that time) and to judge him by these foolish youthful acts instead of by those actions which make him worthy of entering history as the only one who wanted to shoot Hitler? But this is what counts most of all: we have no idea, do we, what else Bavaud thought and said about politics. We don't know it because his executioners had closed his mouth already two years before they cut off his head. He was prohibited from making any kind of political confession. What then allows us to exploit, spitefully and after the fact (as Urner does), the incident that Bavaud temporarily subscribed to a stupid anti-Semitic journal? Because otherwise, thanks to the Nazis, we know *nothing* about him.

All that can be proved is that the man who wanted to shoot Hitler from the honorary grandstand no longer felt that he needed to follow his fellow student Gerbohay's instructions to ask Hitler about the war he was waging against "Bolshevism." No, Bavaud wanted to shoot, nothing else. We can also ascertain that Bavaud's alleged anti-Semitism (which Urner blindly and furiously uses against him) did *not* motivate the Swiss confederate to ally himself with Hitler the day after the latter's "Crystal Night." Rather, it kept Bavaud unerringly on his course to kill Hitler. If Bavaud had been an anti-Semite (yes, it is true he grouched about the alleged exploitation in Jewish as well as non-Jewish department stores), if he had been an anti-Semite like the Nazis, he would not have set out to shoot *the* most consistent killer of Jews in history! And there is no doubting *that*.

Which is why we should stick to that, because otherwise we have awfully little to go on. For the Nazis were masters at putting their opponents out of commission, of trotting out political confessions from their prisons. . . . Bavaud's uncle Gutterer was state secretary of the Minister for Propaganda Goebbels who, until Himmler became effective during the war, was the most horrible of all anti-Semites. What could have prevented Maurice Bavaud from becoming an anti-Semitic writer from Switzerland? After all, he had all the qualifications and connections: he was young and blond and Aryan looking, he appeared to be a journalist, and he had an uncle who was a noted fellow traveler of the anti-Semite Goebbels. Urner, however, cultivates the method of not evaluating his material, and so as to anger Urner once more, I consciously repeat: Bavaud was a lonely *hero* by his intent, which would have been the equivalent of freeing half a continent had he succeeded. But Urner measures him by youthful drivel of which he delivered himself in clerical and therefore *invariably* anti-Semitic circles and dormitory halls. What would it be like if Professor Hoffman (of Stuttgart and Montreal), who is writing the authoritative Stauffenberg biography, who first came on Bavaud's tracks, were to treat the gallant officer the way Urner treats Bavaud and ignore his deed on July 20, 1944, and judge him solely by his trust in Hitler and his enthusiasm for him at the beginning of the thirties!

Urner is mad when he thinks that of all people a staunch anti-Semite would plan to kill Hitler. No one is an instant anti-Semite who vociferates once in his limitation and hatred — today against Jews, tomorrow about Germans, or Frenchmen, Christians or farmers, capitalists or communists. In his naïveté Urner also misinterprets Bavaud's few months' membership in the organization "Front National," whose program was "*contre le marxisme, le communisme, le bolchevisme qui mène à la guerre civile et la révolution.*" Bavaud was only an apprentice at the time who wanted to commit himself, and who searched wherever he could as every intellectually alive adolescent does when he is bored in his small hometown. There leads no direct line from this fellow-traveling of just a few months at age seventeen to the decision to kill Hitler, which is the only interesting decision that Bavaud made for posterity and for his entire life. The intelligent — Urner cusses him as "naïf" — Bavaud saw very soon that he was not a member of that "front," and declared that he was leaving, so as to go on *searching* where he belonged. What a normal, what a harmless thing for a youngster to do! And how should Maurice have known in October 1938 when he subscribed to Fleischhauer's hate sheet, published in Erfurt, Thuringia, what the index-file owner Urner knows today about anti-Semitism, what he knows only *after* Auschwitz. I repeat: all of us only know about the consequences which anti-Semitism *can* have when a Hitler practices as the master of Europe. How do we know who told Maurice about it, what his real purpose in subscribing was?

But are we allowed to denounce Maurice because we know about consequences which happened only when Maurice was long in prison? How totally incapable Urner is of empathizing with Bavaud's motives becomes absolutely clear from this remark: "Evidently so as to while away his time on the evening of November 11, he [Bavaud] still wrote a Latin commentary on his rented typewriter: 'De Judeis. — Judei mundi mala sunt.' . . ."

We can find the words in the indictment. But let me add this to Urner's suspicion. Bavaud did not begin to write his observation so as to "evidently while away his time." We know that he rented this machine because he had been unable to get a shot off on November 9 and had heard that the easiest way of getting close to the Führer was by means of a letter of recommendation. We also know that he had represented himself to these German professors as a stringer for Swiss newspapers. It so happened that anti-Semitism was *the* most discussed subject in Germany during these days following the pogrom against the Jews. What could be more obvious than that Bavaud would seize upon it when he prepared himself to approach Hitler with a forged letter? What lay closer at hand when he started to compose his essay, which was written in the anti-Semitic spirit of the Nazis, than to want to prove how he wanted to write from Germany for the Swiss press? He had to expect that someone who would introduce him to Hitler (it was absurd to expect, but that was what Bavaud hoped for) would ask him to show an article on which he was working? What else — after the "Crystal Night" — should an "admirer" of the terrorist Hitler have proffered as proof that he was an enthusiastic supporter of the Führer's actions against the Jews and that by profession he was a journalist? Why else should Bavaud write this anti-Semitic note and nothing else, not even a letter to his parents, at a time when he was making preparations for the assassination and his own imminent demise. Because, of course, it was absolutely clear to him that he would be killed on the spot if he ever succeeded. The only reason Bavaud wrote this essay was because he believed that he needed it for the assassination, as his I.D.! That, I suspect, is why he wrote it after he had completed his forged letter . . . not "to while away his time": for that his life was far too tense during these hours of highest danger. . . .

But why didn't he explain that to the Gestapo? This is the moment when we have to break off and admit that we cannot say anything more about Bavaud, because without question he was horribly tortured before he (and this remains suspiciously inexplicable and unmotivated) made his confession, to which no evidence but only torture could have brought him. What else could have done it? Why — without being tortured — should he have confessed?

We have at least one piece of evidence that it went something like that, and that is the report by Schellenberg, the head of Himmler's secret service, about the interrogations to which the assassin Georg Elser was subjected the same year and for the same reason. What horrors must have transpired during these "interrogations," such horrors that even the by no means squeamish intimate of Heydrich, Himmler and Müller, Walter Schellenberg, was overcome by dread. And if one reads what Schellenberg writes (see footnote 12), one can conclude only that Bavaud, like Elser, when confronted by the same beaters, reached the same conclusion: he had to interest these beaters in preserving his life if he was not to be beaten to death on the spot. Therefore Bavaud and Elser invented — the former in his recollections of Gerbohay, the latter out of sheer fantasy — nearly the same kinds of stories about accomplices. These stories kept their interrogators on tenterhooks, invariably led to further interrogations that prolonged their lives, and finally really did make the interrogators "save" Bavaud for many months, up to a trial at which the dignity of his person again became commensurate with the great dignity of his act, and he admitted having acted alone. Elser with his fairy-tale about accomplices succeeded in saving his life until the end of the war. Although the Gestapo no longer doubted that Elser had acted alone after he had reconstructed his time bomb, Hitler in the meantime had fabricated the plan to exhibit Elser, after the "final victory," as an alleged tool of the British secret service. . . .

The fact that Urner denounces Bavaud for his "naïve foolhardiness" in not making sure before his trip from Baden-Baden (at

Gutterer's) that Hitler was in Berlin only proves that Urner has no idea how difficult it could be even for someone as well informed as Stauffenberg to make such inquiries. For example, Stauffenberg twice had to take his explosives back home with him, once from Obersalzberg, once from the Wolfsschanze, because to his surprise neither Göring nor Himmler, whom he had wanted to kill together with Hitler, was present. And Stauffenberg had connections to friends from Hitler's closest circle! One should therefore be that much more astonished at how close Bavaud, the foreigner who did not speak German and who had no information whatsoever, was able to get to the animal from the deep! Where limitless sympathy, where the highest admiration for the well-honed intelligence of this young man are in order, his compatriot has only scorn and snootiness. But that is why he was also allowed to write his "report" in three issues of that *Neuen Züricher Zeitung*! Thomas Mann already wrote his brother Heinrich on July 2, 1935, what still holds true of that paper's commentaries on contemporary affairs even today: "The conduct of the bourgeois world press, i.e., the *NZZ*, with respect to such events is unspeakably low."

Before readers, especially younger ones who no longer know what language must be used under dictatorships even by the highest dignitaries who want to get a hearing with the beasts, read the indictment and death sentence against Bavaud, they should learn from the *Memoirs* of Hitler's undersecretary of the Foreign Office, Weizsäcker, what he secretly noted down in 1944 regarding the question of guilt: "If scholars use the sources of the Third Reich, they should consider that no one in Germany at that time was able to achieve his objective if he did not accommodate himself to the dominant forms of expression. . . . These sources are scarcely usable historically without knowledge of the main and secondary recipients. Anyone who wanted to be politically effective at that time did not write so as to appear later as the person who was in the right, or to save his soul. That person was talking and writing in competition with psychopaths and for psychopaths. Historians will recognize that. They will not stop at the slogans that are valid today. . . ."

Weizsäcker had to remain silent but he said to his trusted friend Erich Kordt before the beginning of the war, because he had realized with despair that Hitler's lust for war could not be reined in by any argument: "Do you have a man with a pistol? I regret that it was not part of my education to kill a human being." The fact that the same Weizsäcker, when the confederate Bavaud, the "man with the pistol," had stood before his judges, spoke very coolly with Bern's ambassador, Frölicher, about Bavaud (we print it here) proves only once again how dictators finally make even people with the best intentions and knowledge into accomplices.

With Weizsäcker's words in our ears we should also never forget when we read the indictment that Bavaud was sitting here in front of people to whom he had admitted that he had wanted to murder the (at the time) indescribably popular and worldwide respected Führer of the Germans, that he was bound and tortured and presumably shivering with fear. Bavaud, however he may appear to us in these Nazi files, is no longer himself. To contemplate this and never to forget it is the least service we can pay him when we read these files which were prepared by the most monstrous justice machine known to history. The files originated in the archives of the Berlin Foreign Office, whence they were sent because Bavaud was a foreigner. Here — signature illegible — a report by Dr. Crohne about the question whether members of the Swiss embassy should be present during the proceedings against Bavaud:

The Reich Minister of Justice
III g¹⁰ᵃ 806ᵃ/39 g

> Berlin W 8, November 23, 1939
> Wilhelmstrasse 65
> Tel: 11 00 44

> Express Letter

To
the *Foreign Office*

Re: Criminal Case against the Swiss National Maurice Bavaud
II J 149/39 g of the Reich State Attorney Office at the People's
Court   Secret!

The Reich Attorney General at the People's Court has indicted the *Swiss* national Maurice Bavaud because of a crime
against § 5 of the Decree of the President of the Reich for Protection of the People and the State of February 28, 1933 (RGB1.
I S. 83). Because of the nature of the proceedings I may be
permitted to refer to the copy of the indictment which the Attorney General at the People's Court has sent to you. The trial
will presumably take place on December 18, 1939 before the
2nd Senate of the People's Court.

I am imminently expecting a decision by the Führer, whom I
have to keep current on this matter, about the question whether
the public and the press may be admitted to the trial. A pretrial
hearing in this matter is to take place
on Monday, November 27, 1939 at 12 noon

at the Reich Ministry of Justice, Room Nr. 142 (rear building) to which I ask you to sent a representative.

> By order of Dr. Crohne
> [stamp]

> Certified
> Ministerial secretary
> [signature illegible]

Pol II. Ref. Ges. Rat Auer.

As representative of the Foreign Office I participated at the conference in the RJM (Chairman, Ministerial Director Crohne m. Pro. Mi. Gestapo-Representatives). The question was whether the trial of Bavaud should be conducted in *public*. There was unanimous agreement that a public trial would be inappropriate, because this would inform the public of the relative ease of assassination attempts and might also provide details of other assassination attempts. With regard to the effect of the dissemination of the news of assassinations abroad and the possible incitment to further attempts I also opposed publicly held trials as not in the interest of the Foreign Office.

It remained an open question whether a representative of the Swiss embassy could participate in the *closed* trial. RJM, however, expressed the urgent wish to reject such a possible request by the embassy, as has been done previously in other cases with the Danish embassy.

> [signature illegible]

Reich Attorney General   Berlin W 9, November 23, 1939
at the People's Court   Bellevuestrasse 15
                                     Tel: 21 83 41

Sign: II J 49/39 g
(Please use with your reply)

                                                    Foreigner!
                                                    Registered!

The Foreign Office
To the Hands of Counselor Schipke
or Deputies in the Office at
Berlin W 8
Wilhelmstrasse 76

Re: Proceedings against the Swiss National Maurice Bavaud
    from Neuchâtel
    because of crimes against § 5 No. 1 of the decree for the
    protection of the People and the State of February 28, 1933
    — RGB1. I S. 83 — (undertaking to kill the Führer)

Enclosure:
I am enclosing a copy of my indictment of November 20, 1939.

                            By order of Dr. Nugel
                            [stamp]

                                        certified
                                        Chancellory employee

Reich Attorney General
at the People's Court

Berlin, November 20, 1939

Secret!

Prison! Foreigner!

II J. 149/39 g

= volume I
= volume II
= volume III
= appendix volume
= supplement

Indictment

The technical draftsman Maurice Bavaud, born on January 15,
1916 in Neuchâtel (Switzerland), and still residing there, a
Swiss National, unmarried, was sentenced by the Civil Court
Augsburg on December 6, 1938 — Cs 1729/38 — for illegal
possession of a weapon and fraud to two months and one week
in prison,

provisionally arrested on November 13, 1938, then detained
in the above-mentioned matter from November 24, 1938, until February 14, 1939, subsequently under police arrest for
the matter in question and since March 1, 1939 — at Investigative Prison Berlin Alt-Moabit — under investigative
detention,

— so far without defense attorney —

I accuse,

in October and November 1938 in Baden-Baden, Berlin,
Berchtesgaden, Munich and Bischofswiesen having continu-

ously sought to kill the Führer and Reich Chancellor, Crime against § 5 No. 1 of the Decree of the Reich President for the Protection of the People and the State of February 28, 1933 (RGBl. I S 83).

In October 1938 in Baden-Baden the accused volunteered to kill the Führer and Reich Chancellor, and from October 20 until November 12, 1938, sought to perform this deed. So as to achieve his purpose he tried to reach the immediate vicinity of the Führer in Berlin, Berchtesgaden, Munich and Bischofswiesen. In this process he managed to obtain an honorary ticket for a grandstand seat in Munich to observe the memorial procession on November 9, 1938, then also occupied the grandstand seat and waited with a loaded pistol for an opportunity to get off a shot at the Führer. The only reason he desisted from translating his plan into action while the procession with the Führer and his old party comrades marched past, was because the distance seemed too great for him to shoot his pistol. The planned alternative methods of performing the assassination ultimately failed because the defendant despite his repeated and stubborn attempts was unable to reach the appropriate vicinity of the Führer which would have allowed him to get off accurate pistol shots.

The Finding of the Investigation
I
The Personal Situation of the Defendant

The defendant is the oldest son of the postal official Alfred Bavaud and his wife Helene, née Steiner, in Neuchâtel (Switzerland). His father there holds a position which corresponds to that of a German mail carrier first class. The mother of the defendant maintains a fruit and vegetable shop. The defendant assessed his father's monthly income at between 400 and 500 Swiss francs, while estimating the monthly turnover of his mother's shop at roughly 6000 Swiss francs, of which 10 to 20 percent is profit. The defendant has five siblings, of which one brother and one sister are employed in the mother's shop and another sister has a job as a salesgirl in Neuchâtel, while the youngest brother and sister still attend school.

The defendant's grandmother, Leopoldine Steiner, née Nofaier, who also lives in Neuchâtel, is the sister of Karoline Gutterer, née Nofaier, the wife of the retired superintendent Peter Gutterer who lives in Baden-Baden. The defendant attended grade school in Neuchâtel from age six to fourteen, briefly afterwards the secondary school in the same town, and subsequently the technical institute in Freiburg (Switzerland). Around May 1932 he began an apprenticeship as a draftsman at the Favag firm, in Neuchâtel, and after completing his training in 1935 was also employed there for two months. During his student days he joined the St. Josef Association, which included youths between the ages of 16 and 25, was led by a vicar at the time, and which, beside religious exercises, was devoted to sports and social games.

During the last years of his apprenticeship the defendant became a member of the Neuchâtel chapter of the party Front National. The defendant allegedly decided to join this party, which according to him expresses a Nationalist Swiss political direction with anti-Semitic and anti-democratic ideas, after reading political articles in newspapers. After six or seven months, however, the defendant gave up his membership in this so-called party because the local leadership left something to be desired, and because, in the meantime, he had reached the *decision* to become a *missionary*, having been motivated by a book which describes the life of a missionary in the Congo. This book also is supposed to have contained the suggestion that the "Congregation de Saint Esprit," whose main seat is in Paris, trains missionaries. Since his profession as a technical draftsman no longer satisfied him, he allegedly turned to this address, and soon after had a conversation with a missionary society priest in Neuchâtel, during which he had to show the priest identification about himself and his family. After information had been gathered from the Catholic priest in Neuchâtel, the defendant says that he was ordered to go to a chapter of the missionary society in Freiburg (Switzerland) where, after a short test, he was informed that he would be sent to the seminary in St. Brieuc. The missionary society expressed its willingness to assume the share of his educational costs, so that the parents needed only to contribute the annual boarding fee of approximately 100 Swiss francs. The training was to take the following course: four years of preparation for the missionary profession; and afterwards, as a member of the society, a special seven-year course, in the sixth year of which the defendant was to become a member of the priesthood.

The defendant began his preparatory training at the St. Brieuc Seminary in October 1935. The first year agreed with him, especially the history courses, which are also said to have included discussions about the political situation, not that the teachers took a firm political line themselves. The defendant claims not to have noticed outright opposition to National Socialism and Fascism in the seminary. In the lectures and prayers the teachers took a very hard line only against *Bolshevism*. However, beginning with the second year, the defendant began to lose pleasure in the seminary because its strict regimen, of which the seminary made a special point, interfered with his old and far freer habits. Therefore, he said, he realized during the third year that he was not cut out to be a priest or a missionary, and decided in July 1938, during a vacation with his parents in Neuchâtel, not to return to St. Brieuc, conveying this news by letter to his seminary leader in St. Brieuc. Soon thereafter, the defendant's confessor from St. Brieuc is said to have paid a visit to the parents to double check the defendant's decision with them. The defendant himself, however, happened to be away at the time. According to the defendant, neither the seminary leaders nor the missionary society undertook further attempts to persuade him to change his mind.

After the defendant returned from St. Brieuc to his parents in Neuchâtel he vainly tried to find a job in his profession as technical draftsman. Instead he worked in his mother's store and claims to have received free board and room as well as 50 francs a month as salary. Since his parents' apartment was too small, he found lodging with one of his father's sisters, Adeline Bavaud, to whom, he said, he paid the monthly rent of 15 francs.

The defendant said that he did not renew his contacts with the Swiss party Front National after his return from St. Brieuc.

Beside working in his mother's store, the defendant busied himself learning German and Russian, with the intention, if necessary, of moving to Germany or Russia to find a job as a technical draftsman. However his knowledge of German does not suffice for him to make himself comprehensible in that language.

II

Presentation of the Facts

The defendant claims that after his return from St. Brieuc his anti-Semitic and anti-democratic sentiments were heightened by his reading of political reports in Swiss dailies. What chiefly contributed to the development of this attitude was that most major Swiss dailies were owned by Jews and that the unreliability of their reportage was self-evident from the contradictions in the news reports. This became particularly evident in the reports about the situation of the Sudeten Germans, where contradictions were evident between the German and Swiss news

bureau accounts both of which were broadcast by the Swiss radio station Sottens. This experience led the defendant to decide
to investigate the foundations of National Socialism on his own,
and for this purpose he bought the French edition of *Mein Kampf*
as well as the French collection of the Führer's most important
speeches which is published under the title of *Ma Doctrine*. The
defendant then claims to have been converted to National Socialism and to have wanted to familiarize himself with the conditions in Germany from his own perspective, and to have communicated this wish to a Swiss friend with connections to
National Socialist circles in Germany, whose name, however,
he refuses to divulge. According to the defendant, this friend
then brought him together — around August 1938 — with a
German who was in Neuchâtel, who then acquainted him with
two further Germans and with his future director. All that the
defendant is willing to say about this man, whose name he also
refuses to divulge, is that he is a very influential personality in
Germany who is close to circles around the Führer and a convinced adherent of National Socialism. This last fact especially
influenced the defendant and motivated him to invest unshak-
able trust in this man already during their first discussions. During a second meeting, the defendant said, he communicated the
wish to travel to Germany to his future director, and also mentioned that he had relatives in Baden-Baden whom he could
visit, whereupon the German is supposed to have asked him to
prepare himself for such a trip, because he might conceivably
need him soon in Germany. No exact date for the defendant's
visit was set at that time. His trip was made dependent on the
acquisition of sufficient funds and on his passport being extended. On October 2, 1938, the defendant then ordered a six
months' subscription to the journal *Weltdienst*, and immediately
included the subscription price of 6 Reichsmarks. His letter

accompanying this subscription was written in French and reads
[in translation] as follows:

Neuchâtel, October 2, 1938

"Service Mondial" (Weltdienst)
Daberstedter Strasse 4
Erfurt
Deutschland

Gentlemen,
You don't seem to get many letters from Switzerland, especially
the French-speaking part. But we have a few honorable people
left over too, who are fighting the machinations of Judah. As I
heard, your journal is closely watched by the democracy, which
makes it that much more interesting. I admire your efforts,
gentlemen, which I would like to support actively. Since I cannot do more here, I would like to take out a six-month subscription to your journal for a start.

Respectfully yours,
[signed] Maurice Bavaud
20 rue de Seyon, Neuchatel

P.S. In recent times the Jews have become really afraid, afraid
of Germany. Enclosed you will find a postal order in the amount
of 6 RM.

Soon after October 2, the defendant claims he was looked up by
a man whom he supposely already met in company of the German with whom he had the aforementioned conversation. This
man supposedly asked the defendant when he would come to
Germany, whereupon they arranged the date of October 9,
1938, for his departure for Baden-Baden. On October 4, 1938,

he then had his passport extended to November 4, 1938, and he acquired the necessary funds for his trip on the night of October 9, 1938, by searching out the second key to his mother's safe in his mother's store and taking an amount of approximately 600 Swiss francs from it. Thereupon he drove from Neuchâtel to Basel sometime between 6 and 7 A.M. on Sunday, October 9, 1938, leaving behind a note in his parents' home whose translation from the French reads as follows:

"Dear Parents, don't worry about me, I'm going to build myself an existence. Maurice."

The defendant arrived in Basel between 9 and 10 A.M. and immediately went to the exchange booth of the Dresdner Bank and for the money in his possession, 538.35 Swiss francs, acquired a letter of credit in the amount of 555 RM. Thereafter he took the train to Baden-Baden where he arrived around 2 P.M. Immediately after his arrival the defendant went to the apartment of his great-aunt, Frau Karoline Gutterer, whom he met in the company of her husband. He introduced himself as the grandson of her sister, and explained that he had come to Germany for the express purpose of looking for work in his profession as a technical draftsman. On the day of the defendant's arrival the Gutterers happened to be visited by their nephew, the foreman Karl Gutterer, and his family, with whom the defendant discussed the political situation, expresed his anti-Semitic sentiments and his admiration of the Führer and the achievements of National Socialism. To the question how much money he had the defendant proffered his letter of credit. So as to help him find a job, the stepdaughter of the Gutterers, the salesgirl Paula Gutterer, checked with the employment office in Baden-Baden for a suitable job for the defendant, which office suggested to her to get in touch with the equivalent office in Rastatt. On

October 11 she and the defendant then traveled to Rastatt, taking along his vita which she had written down from comments he had made. In Rastatt they looked up an official of the employment office with whom Paula Gutterer was acquainted, who immediately called the firm Daimler-Benz for a job for the defendant but received the reply that the company was not allowed to hire foreigners. Thereupon all three drove to the Stierlen Works where the official and the defendant approached management and then returned to the waiting Paula Gutterer with the news that there was a likelihood that the defendant would get a job there, but that they had to wait for written confirmation. Thereupon Paula Gutterer and the defendant returned to Baden-Baden where he received a negative reply from the Stierlen Works on October 19, 1938.

In the meantime, the defendant continued to stay with the Gutterers. On October 10, 1938, he withdrew 50 RM against his letter of credit, so as to have pocket money for his own purposes. He spent most of his days going for walks, telling his relatives that he was going to town to send a few postcards. He was always punctually at home for meals; on the other hand, he evinced little interest in attending Catholic church services. When his relatives asked him to attend church on October 16, 1938, and described the church's location to him, they eventually persuaded him to leave the apartment, but he returned quickly, saying that he had been unable to find the church. This seemed particularly strange to Frau Gutterer and to her stepdaughter Paula as they knew that their Swiss relatives were strict churchgoing Catholics.

Frau Gutterer had informed her son Leopold Gutterer, who worked at the Ministry for Enlightenment and Propaganda, of the defendant's visit already on the day of his arrival. Her son found the sudden visit by the defendant, with whose family there had been no contact for years, particularly surprising since the defendant had mentioned his profession as technical draftsman and was looking for a job in Germany. As it seemed more than likely that the defendant had entered Germany with the express purpose of reconnoitering the construction of the fortifications being built in the West at that time, Director Leopold Gutterer informed the Gestapo of defendant's arrival, and on October 15 also sent his wife to his parents in Baden-Baden with the mission, if necessary, to warn them against the defendant and to make sure that the defendant while looking for work should under no circumstances avail himself of his, the director's, name as a recommendation. So as to lend her visit to her relatives as innocuous an appearance as possible, the wife of director Gutterer took along her six-year-old son, Dietrich. There, in Baden-Baden, she then fulfilled her mission but herself was unable to engage the defendant in a conversation since she does not know French. On the other hand, the defendant frequently took the child along on his walks in and around Baden-Baden.

While in Baden-Baden the defendant informed his parents that he was staying with relatives there, and also admitted to them the theft of the money from the safe, asking them not to mention it in a possible letter to the relatives in Baden-Baden, since this might demean him in their eyes. He also wrote to his friend Gerbohay from the seminary in St. Brieuc and told him he was in Germany, whereupon the latter sent him a reply care of the Gutterers which, however, did not arrive until October 29, 1938, when the defendant had already left Baden-Baden. Since the defendant was already under, if only vague, suspicion due to the warning issued by Director Gutterer, and nothing was known about his current whereabouts, the Gutterers gave the letter to the Gestapo, which opened it, had it translated from the French, and then forwarded it to the defendant's parents in

Neuchâtel. The translation of this letter, on which one could make out the postmark "Château Giron Ille-et-Vilaine," goes as follows:

Dear Maurice!
Your postcards, your letters made me very happy. What you tell me about Germany does not astonish me in the least. I'm afraid that this admiration will bring harm to the good of your soul. Be careful, and in everything chiefly follow God's commandments. Know that no person can disobey them without being punished. God sees everything, he also sees you and watches over you. It seems to me that you doubt that and consider it your duty to communicate these doubts in certain writings which cannot possibly be from your pen. That is what frightens me. Germany is certainly great, but isn't that God? God the Almighty. He can diminish Germany, just as he has enlarged it. Never forget that, so that this thought may heal you and make you follow God's commandments.

Excuse the brevity of this letter, you know the reasons why. Until soon I hope.

Your friend in Christ, Marcel.

The defendant also accepted letters at the Baden-Baden post office which had been sent there *poste restante* under his name. However, it can no longer be ascertained where they came from.

During the walks which the defendant took by himself in Baden-Baden, he claims that on three different days, the first time already the day after his arrival, he met with the man at whose suggestion he had come to Germany. Once this man was by himself, the other two times in company of two other men, one of whom is supposed to have been the defendant's director with whom the defendant arranged the date of his arrival in Germany shortly after October 2, 1938. According to the defendant, the main topic of conversation during these discussions in Baden-Baden is supposed to have been the political situation. During these discussions the director, in whom the defendant claims to have invested unlimited trust already in Neuchâtel, is supposed to have expressed his dissatisfaction with the Führer's peace policy: now that the Führer so generously had made the *Wehrmacht* so strong that France and England were forced to accept his conditions in Munich, it should be used to realize pan-Germanic ideas in a war. However, the person of the Führer, who had always pursued a policy of peace, stood in the way of such a policy. The defendant claims that he immediately saw that such an assessment of the situation was the only correct one for a National Socialist, and immediately offered to kill the Führer himself. Thereupon the spokesman of the three Germans is supposed to have commissioned him to assassinate the Führer and advised him to buy himself a pistol in Switzerland, since he would be able to obtain it there without a gun permit. Then the defendant was to go to Berlin where he would meet him on Sunday October 22, 1938, at the Faun Theater in the Friedrichstrasse. Furthermore, defendant claims that it was during this meeting that he received the note with his director's handwriting on it, which reads as follows:

"Cet homme est sous ma protektion immediate et n'a rien fait qui ne soit selon mes ordres."

Which in translation states:

"This man stands under my immediate protection and has done nothing which does not conform to my orders."

Beneath this text we find three intertwined letters, which evidently present an *A*, an *H*, and a *B* with a line drawn through them. While handing him this note, the director is supposed to have said that its content might seem childish to him, but that he should always carry it with him; which is why the defendant considered this piece of writing a special declaration of protection. The defendant said that he did not receive any funds from his director who, however, knew the amount the defendant carried on himself. The defendant declared that it was important to him to defray the cost of this act with his own means since the final decision to kill the Führer stemmed from his own supposedly idealistic motives, which is why he did not want to receive any remuneration for this act.

As the sum that was presumably needed for his trip to Switzerland and for the acquisition of a pistol, the defendant, on October 17, 1938, had the branch of the Dresdner Bank in Baden-Baden give him 100 RM against his letter of credit. On the same day he explained to his relatives that he wanted to go to Mannheim to discuss the question of obtaining a job in Germany with the Swiss consulate. So that the relatives would not accompany him, he added that he would take the streetcar to the Baden-Oos railroad station. He then took his luggage to the railroad station, and had the railway ship it directly to the Berlin Anhalter railroad station. He himself took the train to Basel.

After his arrival in Basel the defendant immediately looked up the shop of gunsmith Bürgin, Am Steinentor 13, and bought himself a pistol (Schmeisser, 6.35mm) and 10 bullets, for approximately 30 francs. Thereupon he returned to the main railroad station in Basel and withdrew 50 RM against his letter of credit from the branch of the Dresdner Bank there, after which he took the train to Berlin where he arrived on October 21, 1938. At first he tried to find a furnished room in the center of the city, but when he did not succeed the defendant decided to stay one night in the hotel Alexandra in the Mittelstrasse. There he immediately registered himself with the police under his own name on an appropriately filled out form and then took his baggage, which was waiting for him at the Anhalter railroad station, to the hotel.

On the morning of October 22, 1938 he went again in search of a furnished room. He had seen a room in the Kaiserallee advertised in a newspaper and therefore drove to that part of the city. While walking through the Berliner Strasse around 1:30 P.M. he then saw a sign at number 146 offering a furnished room, whereupon he looked up the apartment and was received by its proprietor, the pensioner Anna Radke, to whom he signified in broken German, using the words "room," "free," "at once," that he wanted to take the room right away. Further communication between them was then conducted with the pensioner Radke writing her questions and answers on a piece of paper, which the defendant read, because it was easier for him to read than to speak German. To Frau Radke's question what his job was he replied traveling salesman. He immediately agreed to the monthly rent of 35 RM and at once paid the 13 RM for the remaining days of October, as well as 2 RM for the cost of lighting. He also offered to pay the rent for November but Frau Radke declined to accept the money, giving as her reason that she wanted him first to occupy the room in October; and she replied to his question, whether he could occupy the room the same day, that he could do so after 4 P.M., by which time it would be it in order. Thereupon the defendant returned to the inner city where he bought a further 25 bullets, caliber 6.35mm, at a weapons shop near the Friedrichstrasse, which were handed him without further ado since the buying of ammunition is under no restrictions for persons over 18 years of age. At which point the accused took his luggage from the hotel Alexandra, and arrived around 4:30 P.M. at Frau Radke's apartment. Frau Radke called his immediate attention to the fact that he had to register with the police, and from the balcony of her apartment pointed out the location of the local police precinct. After he had made himself at home in his furnished room, he left the apartment the same afternoon and returned around 7:00 P.M. with the police registry forms, which he had brought. That evening and night the defendant stayed in his room, and on the following Sunday, October 23, 1938, he left around noon, leaving the filled-out police forms behind in his room, which the pensioner Radke took and signed as the landlady.

The defendant claims that he then kept his prearranged date with his director at the Faun Theater in the Friedrichstrasse, where the latter told him that the Führer presently was not in Berlin and that he should go to Berchtesgaden, where his chances of meeting the Führer were far greater. The defendant claims to have been of the opinion that his director was always informed about the Führer's whereabouts. The defendant returned to his furnished room that evening and did not leave it until 9 A.M. Monday morning, October 24, 1938. At this time he left his room with his luggage and, upon encountering Frau Radke in the hallway of the apartment, told her that he was going to Dresden for five days. He made this comprehensible to her by raising the five fingers on one hand and saying: "five . . . days . . . trip . . . Dresden." Frau Radke thereupon replied that he still had to register with the police before leaving, and handed him the filled-out forms. The defendant assured her that he would do so at once and then declared that he wanted to leave the house key behind because it was too big for him. However, the defendant turned down Frau Radke's request also to leave the apartment keys behind. When she said he could ring the bell upon his return and she would open for him, he turned down her suggestion with the remark that he wanted to keep the keys since he would be returning in five days anyway. The defendant did not want to reveal the actual destination of his trip

several walks in the surrounding area and used these walks to train himself to shoot a pistol, for which purpose he fired approximately 25 shots from a distance of seven or eight meters at trees. Furthermore, he once tried to gain admittance to the Berghof, inquiring from a policeman on the street how he might approach this objective. The official explained to him that there was no way of approaching the vicinity of the Berghof on the Obersalzberg without first passing through the blockade. The defendant then asked the manager of the hotel Stiftskeller whether he knew someone in Berchtesgaden who knew French. Manager Zeitter got the impression from the defendant's inquiry that he had become bored in Berchtesgaden without being able to talk to someone, and called his attention to the fact that Professor Ehrenspeck, who taught at the Berchtesgaden High School, knew French. He suggested to the defendant that he should look him up, whereupon the defendant had himself taken to Professor Ehrenspeck during school hours, introduced himself to him and told him that Berchtesgaden bored him because he knew too little German and wanted to become acquainted with people who spoke French. Ehrenspeck thereupon talked to him and noticed to his astonishment that the defendant had not gone to the Königsee despite the fact that he had been in Berchtesgaden already several days. He arranged to meet the defendant the following afternoon at the Café Rottenhöfer, to which meeting he also brought along Professor Reuther who also taught at the high school. The conversation at first touched on political conditions in France, during which the defendant compared the French parliamentary system in an entirely unobtrusive manner with the German authoritarian system, emphasizing the advantages of the latter. It was in this connection that he expressed the wish to see and meet the Führer, adding that he had come to Berchtesgaden for this very purpose. Ehrenspeck and

Reuther explained to him that it was scarcely possible to speak to the Führer, but since Major Decket, who worked at the Reich Chancellory and with whom Ehrenspeck was acquainted, happened to be in the coffeehouse, the professor turned to him with the explanation that he was sitting with a young Swiss who seemed to come from a good family and who wanted to see the Führer. Major Deckert replied that it was impossible to see the Führer at present, since he was so busy that even the Reichsministers von Ribbentropp and Dr. Lammers had not been received by him, but it could certainly be assumed that the Führer would be present during the festivities in Munich on November 8 and 9. Ehrenspeck conveyed this piece of information from Major Deckert to the defendant and also took the opportunity to tell him that he himself had gotten the best view of the Führer during the November 9 memorial march by awaiting the arrival of the procession in the Café City and stepping out onto the street only then. Furthermore, he explained that a meeting with the Führer was highly unlikely unless he had an introduction from an influential person. Professor Reuther added that arranging for a meeting with Reichsminister Lammers beforehand would facilitate such a meeting. Ehrenspeck and Reuther then asked the defendant during a second meeting with him, which occurred on one of the following days at the hotel Zur Post, to make himself available for a language lesson at the high school, giving as their reason for this request that they wanted students to meet someone whose mother tongue was French. This would familiarize them with the rhythms and pronunciation of that language. The defendant fulfilled this wish and took part in the French language courses taught by Ehrenspeck and Reuther on October 31, 1938. He read from the school's French textbook and subsequently conducted a dialogue in French with the professors about the distribution of language areas in Switzerland.

At the end of the lesson the defendant departed from the two professors with the remark that he would be leaving Berchtesgaden the same day.

In fact he took a train on October 31, 1938, to Munich and took a room in the hotel Stadt Wien there. During the time between November 2 and 4 the defendant claims to have met once again with his director, a meeting which he says he arranged by sending him a letter in Berlin at a post office address known only to him, and asking him to come to Munich to meet him at the Café Luitpold. Two of his director's delegates are then supposedly to have appeared at the appointed time at the Café Luitpold and told him that the director himself could not come. They then arranged for a new meeting during the next few days, at which the director himself did appear. At first the director allegedly berated the defendant for taking too leisurely an approach to the assassination of the Führer and asked him to speed up his actions; at which point the director allegedly pointed out that the memorial march on November 9, 1938, in which the Führer was bound to partake, presented an excellent opportunity. What was also considered during this occasion was the possibility of gaining a entree to the Führer by means of forged letters of introduction from the former French president Flandin or the French National Assembly delegate Taittinger, and performing the assassination during such a meeting. Otherwise, his director is supposed to have left the execution of these details entirely up to the defendant, and merely remarked that he should proceed cautiously. Now the defendant tried to buy a ticket for the grandstand on November 9, 1938, at several offices, among them the Munich City Hall, the Foreign Press Bureau, and the Watch by the Feldherrnhalle, but was turned away everywhere with the remark that no further tickets were available. However, in the course of his endeavors it was pointed out to the defendant that he might be able to obtain a ticket at the

Official Bureau for November 9, which is why he went to its main office and informed manager Senftinger of his wish. Since Senftinger did not know French he used reporter Bintz, the manager of the Foreign Newspaper Bureau in Munich, who happened to be present, as the translator. The defendant represented himself as a reporter for newspapers in Western Switzerland who, since he had never seen a memorial procession such as the one on November 9, wanted to get a ticket for the grandstand opposite the Heiliggeist Church; he wanted to file a report for the papers he represented. Bintz translated the defendant's wish to Senftinger, who had no further compunctions about handing the defendant a grandstand ticket opposite the Heiliggeist Church, especially since he had several tickets left over. Neither Bintz nor Senftinger asked the defendant for his I.D. In fact, the defendant was the only foreigner who received an honorary ticket for the grandstand.

On one of the following days, probably on November 5, 1938, the defendant bought two packs of bullets, caliber 6.35mm, at the weapons store Abele in Munich, and several practice targets, and also a third pack of bullets at another weapons store whose identity could no longer be ascertained. After the defendant was presented with his hotel bill that day, he felt that he could live more cheaply if he found himself a furnished room in Munich, which is why he gave up his room in the hotel Stadt Wien and went on a search for a furnished room. However, after his search turned out to be fruitless, he returned to the hotel with the remark that he had decided to continue to stay there after all. But since the room in which he had been staying had been let in the meantime, he had to move into a different room.

On the evening of November 5, 1938, the defendant encountered on the Karlsplatz, Professor Reuther from Berchtesgaden, who happened to be in Munich for an air raid practice, and the two of them went to the Café Fahrig. During the course of their conversation the defendant told Reuther that he had had the luck of obtaining a grandstand ticket through the intercession of a foreign newspaper reporter. Around 12 P.M. both of them left the café and walked to the hotel Stadt Wien, where the defendant took leave of the professor.

On Sunday November 6, 1938, the defendant took a trip to Lake Ammensee in the vicinity of Herrsching, rented a boat there and rowed with it out in on to the lake. There he built little paper ships which he set on the water and used for target practice. During one of the following days, probably on November 7, 1938, he took the practice targets he had bought to Pasing, attached them to some trees in a nearby forest, and continued to familiarize himself with the pistol. Altogether he claims that he took approximately 80 practice shots on Lake Ammensee and in Pasing.

After his return to Munich the defendant bought himself a plan of the festivities on November 8 and 9, 1938, from a street vendor, and then inscribed the planned memorial march on a Munich city plan which he had bought previously. Then he walked through the streets through which the procession would pass so as to find the most advantageous spot for the execution of his assassination plan. This led him to the conclusion that the best way of executing his plan would be to station himself inside the Café City, which was situated at a very narrow part of the street, and to step out of the café just before the arrival of the procession. The reason he diverged from this plan was because he already possessed the ticket to the grandstand and believed that if he could get a good seat, he would also be able to perform the assassination there.

The defendant then went so early to the grandstand opposite the Heiliggeist Church on November 9, 1938, that he was assured of receiving a seat in the front row. He kept the loaded pistol in his coat pocket. His plan was to shoot the Führer while the procession moved past the grandstand if there was a high probability of hitting him. When the procession approached and the defendant noticed that the Führer was marching as part of a long row among his comrades, and since he realized the true distance between the grandstand and the procession only now, he reached the conclusion that the pistol shots would not hit the Führer with absolute certainty from his place on the grandstand, but might conceivably hit one of his companions. As the procession marched past, he recognized Field Marshal Göring and Reichsfüherer SS Himmler in the immediate vicinity of the Führer. Since his sole intention was to kill the Führer, and since he did not want to be arrested for wounding someone else, thereby aborting the further execution of his plan, he decided to desist from executing his plan at this moment. He let the entire procession move past and then left the grandstand.

The defendant thereupon returned to the hotel Stadt Wien. Upon further reflection how he was going to commit his planned act, he came upon the idea of gaining entrée to the Führer by means of a forged introduction from the former French president Flandin, and committing the act then. He therefore created a handwritten recommendation and signed it Flandin. He mentioned in this letter of introduction, which he put into an open envelope, that its bearer, Maurice Bavaud, was to personally hand the Führer a letter from the undersigned, the former president of France Flandin. So as to be also safe in the event he was asked for this letter before being admitted to the Führer, he prepared yet a second letter by putting a clean sheet of paper into an envelope, sealing it, and writing the words Reich Chancellor on the front. Thereupon, around noon of November 10, 1938, he drove with the prepared missives once more from Munich to Berchtesgaden, where he arrived between 5 and 6 P.M. So as to reach his objective that much more quickly he took a taxi at the railroad station and told the driver to take him to the

Obersalzberg. The taxi was stopped at the foot to the Obersalzberg at the Schiessstätt Bridge by a guard to whom the defendant explained that he was coming from Paris to personally hand a letter to the Führer. The guard explained to the defendant that he could not admit him to the Berghof, but upon urging by the defendant the guard telephoned the guard on the Berghof, whereupon he informed the defendant that the Führer was not on the Obersalzberg. Using the same taxi, the defendant then drove back to the railroad station and the same evening returned by train to Munich.

The defendant now wanted to try to meet the Führer personally, and this led him to the thought that a handwritten note might arouse suspicion and that it would be better to prepare the letter of introduction as well the address on the typewriter. Therefore he went to the office machine shop of businessman Schrimp in Munich and on November 11, 1938, rented a typewriter there for two days, which was sent to his hotel on the same day. The defendant then wrote a new letter of recommendation on this typewriter, but because he feared that former president Flandin's signature might be known to the Führer personally or to someone in his circle, he now decided to use the recommendation of the French National Assembly delegate Taittinger and to forge his signature. The defendant then also typed the addresses on the envelope. The letter of recommendation reads as follows:

Paris 10 octobre 1938

Excellence

Ayez l'obligeance, je vous prie, de bien vouloir recevoir Monsieur Maurice Bavaud. Je lui ai confié un pli qu'il ne vous remettra qu'en main propre. Il s'agit d'une communication essentiellement privée, bien qu'il y soit question de politique.

Veuillez agréer, Excellence, l'assurance de toute ma considération.

> Pierre Taittinger.
> Député de Paris & président du parti Rép
> National & Soc.

and in its translation:

Your Excellency,
I ask you to be so kind as to receive Mr. Maurice Bavaud. I have entrusted a letter to him which he will hand only to you personally. It is primarily a private matter, though it also touches on politics.
Your Excellency, please be assured of my highest respect.

> Pierre Taittinger
> Delegate from Paris and
> President of the Rep. National
> Soc. Party

The defendant typed the words "Reich Chancellor" on the open envelope of this letter of recommendation. The closed envelope, which merely contained a clean sheet of paper, he marked: "Monsieur le Chancelier Adolf Hitler (aux bons soins de M. M. Bavaud)."

On the evening of November 11, 1938, the defendant also typed the following piece:

"De Judeis. — Judei mundi mala sunt. 'Vae Judae' clamabant romani in bellow judei, Tito duce et Vespasio imperatore. Hoc fuit primo 'pogrom.' Josefus narrat omnes judeos occidi fuerunt, Jerusalem tote deletum fuisse. Aureo penisque judei mundi romani potentia semper fuerunt. Romani nunquam delere vires pernitiosas judeorum potuerunt. Christiani autem" . . .

Which in translation reads:

"About the Jews. — The Jews are the evil of the world. 'Woe to the Jews!' the Romans shouted during the Jewish wars under emperors Titus and Vespasian. This was the first 'pogrom.' Josefus tells us that all Jews were killed and Jerusalem was laid to waste. The Jews always had large masses of gold and money in the Roman world. The Romans were never able to destroy the pernicious power of the Jews. But the Christians" . . .

This piece of writing is supposed to be a result of the defendant's reflection on the occasion of the assassination of ambassadorial counselor vom Rath in Paris. One should not assign any special meaning to it according to him. He claims to have availed himself of Latin simply because he is used to expressing himself in Latin.

On the morning of November 12, 1938, the defendant then went to the "Braune Haus" in Munich with the letter of recommendation and the special envelope for the Führer and with the loaded pistol. At the entrance hall the guard, Hauptsturmführer Koch, asked him what he wanted, whereupon the defendant showed him the letter of recommendation. Since Koch has no command of French he asked the Chancellory employee Miss Hill to join him, who thereupon functioned as the translator during the conversation. The defendant explained that he had to deliver the letter personally to the Führer, whereupon employee Hill translated the letter of recommendation to Hauptsturmführer Koch, who then telephoned the appropriate official expert, Dr. Hanssen, in Reichsleiter Bormann's office, and communicated the defendant's wishes and the content of the letter of recommendation to him. Dr. Hanssen then asked that the defendant be brought to him, whereupon employee Hill led him to the "Haus des Führers." On the way there, the defendant asked whether he was being to taken to see the Führer now, whereupon she replied that he would first be brought to see a gentleman whose task it was to look after these matters for the Führer. When the defendant then said that this must be Rudolf Hess, employee Hill denied this and explained that the gentleman whom he would meet was the expert in matters of this kind. After she had led the defendant into Dr. Hanssen's room, she soon left again. Dr. Hanssen once more inquired after the defendant's wishes and then explained to him that a personal meeting with the Führer was out of the question. After the defendant kept insisting that he had to hand over the letter personally, Dr. Hanssen recommended that he send it by mail or that he leave it with him, who would make sure that the letter would reach the Führer's hands. When the defendant also rejected this proposal and insisted on a personal audience, Dr. Hanssen explained to him that he would have to broach his wishes at the Chancellory. Thereupon the defendant left the "Haus des Führers" and at noon the same day took the train to Bischofswiesen, where he arrived between 5 and 6 P.M. Since all he had left were 5 RM, he decided to walk to the Reich Chancellory on foot, and also asked several persons he met for directions. Since it had become dark in the meantime, it occurred to the defendant that this was not a promising hour to visit the Chancellory, particularly since it was Saturday, and he therefore turned around without having reached his destination and went back to the railroad station Bischofswiesen. So as not to exhaust his funds completely he merely bought a ticket as far as Freilassing and then took a Berchtesgaden train, which stopped in Freilassing, as far as Munich. In Freilassing the wagons of the Berchtesgaden train had been connected to the express Vienna–

"I believe in your star,
We are one body, one heart, one soul,
everywhere and always."

The luggage which the defendant left behind at the hotel Stadt Wien in Munich contained clothing and toilet articles, a national railroad timetable, a map of Munich, a map of the area around Berchtesgaden, writing paper, a leather holster for the pistol and a box of 19 bullets, caliber 6.35mm.

After his arrest on November 24, 1938, the defendant was transferred to the Augsburg Court, which issued an arrest warrant against him for ticket fraud and illegally carrying arms, and which on December 6, 1938, sentenced him to two months and one week of prison, of which one week of investigative detention was applied to the overall sentence. The defendant served his punishment from December 14, 1938, until February 14, 1939.

III
The Defendant's Response

The facts of the case as described in Section II of the indictment are based chiefly on the defendant's own testimony. During his first interrogation by the Gestapo on November 14, 1938, he testified that he came to Germany on October 9, 1938, to become acquainted with conditions in Germany. Further, he declared that he used his savings to buy himself a letter of credit in an amount of more than 500 RM and then stayed for eight to nine days with relatives in Baden-Baden, traveling from there to Berlin to get to know the capital of the Reich. In Berlin he stayed for three or four days at the hotel Alexandra with the intention of seeing the Führer, but then read in a French newspaper that the Führer had gone to Obersalzberg after visiting the Sudetenland, which is why the defendant took a train from Berlin to Berchtesgaden and stayed for about a week in the hotel

Stiftskeller. However, the defendant made no particular attempts to see the Führer there since he had heard that his endeavor would be futile. On October 3, 1938, he then took the train to Munich where he stayed in the hotel Stadt Wien until November 12, 1938. During this period he had wanted to see the Führer during the memorial procession on November 9, 1938, which is why he had gone to several ticket bureaus to obtain a grandstand ticket, which he finally obtained from the Official Bureau for November 9. He then watched the entire procession from his grandstand seat and also saw the Führer. As an alleged admirer of National Socialism and of the Führer he had wanted to talk to him personally and put some questions concerning Switzerland to him, especially regarding its neutrality.

Since it was impossible to meet the Führer in the normal course of events, the idea occurred to him to gain access to him by means of a forged letter of recommendation, which is why he prepared the two forged letters that were found on him. He then went to Bischofswiesen on November 12, 1938, after he had found out that the Reich Chancellory was located there. Since the onset of darkness made it impossible for him to reach the Chancellory and he lacked sufficient funds to be able to continue, he gave up his plan and set out on his return trip, without, however, being able to buy a ticket farther than Freilassing. He then continued his trip without a ticket and was finally taken off the train in Augsburg. To the question why he did not turn to the Swiss consulate in Munich to obtain the necessary funds for his return to Switzerland, he replied that he did not know that he could obtain a ticket in this manner. The defendant further declared during this interrogation that he had already bought the pistol that was found on him, in August in Neuchâtel, out of love for the sport, and always kept it on his person. The defendant decisively denied having had the intent of wanting to talk to the Führer gun in hand. With regard to the note with the declaration of protection that was found on his person, defendant declared on this occasion that the person who wrote the note was a very influential personal in Germany, under whose protection he stood. He refused to give a more detailed account about this matter, explaining that the Gestapo should ascertain for itself the state of affairs of the declaration of protection.

At further Gestapo interrogations between January 24 and 31, 1939, the defendant maintained his previous testimony, only supplementing it with the information that he had sought vainly to find work in Baden-Baden and that in Berlin he spent only one night in the hotel Alexandra, then renting a furnished room. He also admitted having sought to gain admittance to the Führer already in Munich at the "Braune Haus." To the question why he has insisted so stubbornly on a personal interview with the Führer, he explained that if he had succeeded in speaking to him he would have become an "interesting personality." When it was pointed out to him that if he had gained such access the fraudulence of his letter of recommendation would have been recognized at once, the defendant replied that he had counted on that, and would have explained to the Führer that this was the only way to gain access to him; after all, he had heard of the goodness and lovingness of the Führer, he could not imagine that the Führer would hold his approach against him. After renewed questioning about the origin of the note with the declaration of protection, the defendant declared that the note was without any significance whatsoever; he wrote the note himself, without giving further thought to its purpose. After he was asked to provide a sample of his handwriting he however withdrew this explanation and reasserted his previous position that the note had been written by a person of great influence whose protection he enjoyed, but about whom he refused to provide further details. Furthermore, the defendant first maintained his claim that he had bought already the pistol in August 1938. When it was pointed out to him that according to police information he bought the pistol only on October 20, 1938, in Basel and therefore drove from Baden-Baden to Basel, the defendant admitted this and also admitted that he had acquired the funds for his trip to Germany by stealing from his mother, and then, when he failed in his attempt to get a job, became so desperate that he had thought of suicide. Since he knew he could obtain a pistol in Switzerland without a permit, he took the train to Basel and bought a pistol there on October 20, 1938. When it was pointed out to him that this contradicted the fact that he immediately went to Berlin from Basel and only began his stubborn attempts to gain admission to the Führer after he had bought the pistol, the defendant replied: "Le soupçon qu'on a contre moi est un réalité" (What one suspects of me is the truth). admitting what had been suspected, that he had planned to assassinate the Führer. He now made a confession which by and large corresponds to the facts as described in Section II of the Indictment. During the confession, the defendant however continued to refuse to make further revelations about the motives for his act or about the person of his director.

The defendant stuck to this confession during the interrogations to which he was subjected between February 25 and March 1, 1939, only amending it with the revelations about his motives and the meetings with his director as detailed in Section II of the Indictment. He once again refused to name his director or provide further details about him. When he was specifically asked whether he was aware that killing the Führer or an attempt on his life was punishable by death, he admitted this but stated that in his opinion it had not come to an attempt. When it was pointed out to him that according to German law the mere undertaking of such an attempt was already punishable, he explained that he had taken the possibility of any kind of punishment into account and if it had come to an execution of his plan on November 9, 1938 on the grandstand had even counted on the possibility of being lynched by the outraged population. However, he had acted in the belief of complete trust in his director and even now was convinced that he would use his great influence to protect him. When it was pointed out to him that a handwriting analysis by the criminal police had determined that he had written the declaration of protection himself, and that the intertwined letters *A H B* with a line drawn through them should be interpreted as meaning that Adolf Hitler was to be killed by Bavaud, the defendant declared that this analysis was incorrect. He stuck to his version that the handwriting was not his but his director's. The defendant further explained that the letters in the signature on the note contained the initials of his employer, but did not contain an *H*. When it was pointed out to him that the signature at least contained the letters *A* and *B*, the defendant, after looking at the note and the enlargement prepared by the experts, tried to maintain that it could not be a letter *B* since the lower part of the letter was not closed. After it was demonstrated to him that in that case the letter had to be an *R*, the defendant refused to provide any further explanations. When it was pointed out to him that he had already confessed to the police that he had written the note himself, defendant asserted that he had provided this information *before* his actual confession in the hope of deflecting any further questions by the police about the origin of the note. At the time before he confessed to the purpose of his action, he had wanted to avoid shedding any suspicion on his director. Furthermore, he disclaimed having pretended to be a newspaper reporter at the Official Bureau for November 9, or having gone there to obtain a grandstand ticket; he claimed merely to have sought to obtain a program of the festivities. At that point an honorary ticket had been handed to him without his having asked for it. Further, the defendant explained, with regard to the photo of Gerbohay and its dedication in back, that he and Gerbohay had been close friends since their mutual training in St. Brieuc, that they had both exchanged photos with dedications. He said he sent several postcards with greetings to Gerbohay while he was in Germany, the letter from Gerbohay which arrived in Baden-Baden after his departure evidently being a reply. However, he had no explanation for what Gerbohay meant when he wrote of "certain writings which cannot possibly be from your pen," and "excuse the brevity of this letter, you know the reasons why. Until soon I hope." Finally, the defendant decisively rejected the suggestion that he had taken out the subscription to *Weltdienst* and had written the beginning of his essay on the Jews in order to camouflage his actions. He claims to be an opponent of Jewry. Finally, to the question whether he had acted without a director and entirely on his own — especially, in light of his statement during previous interrogations that he had wanted to meet the Führer so as to become an interesting personality — the defendant replied that he was not mad to plan such an act without a serious motive. It was true that he had stated to the police during an earlier interrogation that the above-mentioned motive had been his reason. However this occurred *before* his confession, and had been meant to satisfy the policemen who were looking for a motive for his stubborn attempts to gain access to the Führer, and to keep the police from questioning him further.

When it was pointed out to defendant during the last interrogations on March 27 and 28, 1939, that in the meantime it had been unmistakably ascertained by handwriting analysis that he himself was the writer of the declaration of protection and that the writer was of Romanic and not of Germanic origin, he also claimed that assessment was incorrect and maintained his earlier claims about the origin of the note. The defendant, however, then allowed how the handwriting was very similar to his, and added that in Switzerland, after he had become familiar with his director's handwriting, he had always sought to imitate it, he was so devoted to him, so that a comparison between the two might indeed show a similarity. When it was pointed out to him that the handwriting on the back of the photo of Gerbohay, which was his own, had been used as a basis for the comparison, and that he had not known his director when he had written that dedication, the defendant merely stated that the handwriting expert must be mistaken. The defendant also denied having received mail *poste restante* at the Baden-Baden post office and maintains that the post office officials must be mistaken. Furthermore he disputes statements of the manager of the Official Bureau for November 9 and of reporter Bintz that he passed himself off as a reporter and asked for a grandstand ticket, and declared that these statements must either be in error or based on a mis-identification.

IV

The Factual and Legal Assessment of the Case

The defendant's testimony about his stay in the German Reich and the activities of his which were directed toward an assassination of the Führer have been checked inasmuch as this was possible. The investigation yielded the following results: The defendant did leave Basel on October 9, 1938, taking 600 Swiss francs with him and reached his relatives in Baden-Baden the same day. He stayed there until October 20, 1938, whereupon he traveled to Basel, bought himself a pistol, and traveled to Berlin where he arrived on October 21, 1938, and stayed at the hotel Alexandra the night of October 22, 1938. Until October 24, 1938, he then lived in the furnished room of pensioner Radke. From October 21, 1938, until November 1, 1938, he stayed in the hotel Stiftskeller in Berchtesgaden and made the acquaintance of Professors Ehrenspeck and Reuther. Further, from October 31 until November 12, 1938, he lived in the hotel Stadt Wien in Munich, then bought several packs of bullets and acquired a grandstand ticket from the Official Bureau of November 9. Furthermore, on November 10, 1938, he tried to get past the guard on the Schiessstätt Bridge, referring to his first letter of recommendation to the Obersalzberg, and rented a typewriter on November 11, 1938, in Munich, which was brought to his room in the hotel Stadt Wien the same day. Finally, the defendant approached the "Braune Haus" and the "Haus des Führers" on November 12, 1938, so as to get close to the Führer. Ultimately, upon his arrest, the pistol and the two letters of recommendation were found on the defendant.

The testimony of the defendant about his stay in Germany and his activities relating to his assassination have been checked and have proved to be true; however, the testimony of his which cannot be checked, about his motives for the act and the person of his director, leads to considerable doubts. First of all, it is unbelievable that an allegedly convinced National Socialist should give an order to kill the Führer. The reasons that allegedly motivated him are also unbelievable. And it is completely improbable that a German should of all people have chosen a foreigner, whom he met only a short while before, to execute such a plan. It also speaks against the director's being German that he left the manner of the execution of the plan entirely up to the defendant and kept only the loosest contact with him. What also remains inexplicable is why the defendant, who claims to have been able to arrange meetings with his director upon the shortest of notices in Munich, took the risk of being arrested for ticket fraud because of a lack of funds without having first sought to receive the necessary funds from his allegedly always reachable director, so as to continue the pursuit of his plan or at least so as to prevent the discovery of his previous activities. Finally, the defendant's claim that his declaration of protection, which is in French, was written by his German director is thoroughly disproved by the expert testimony of Dr. Jeserich, according to whom the note was written not only by someone of Romanic origin but most certainly by the defendant himself. Besides, it remains inexplicable why the defendant should think that this declaration of protection, which is in French, should afford him special protection, since it might not be immediately comprehensible to anyone to whom he might show it immediately after an assassination. Finally, the defendant's behavior in Berlin and Munich becomes comprehensible if the meetings he claims took place between him and his director did not occur; for, the news that the Führer was not in the capital could just as easily have been gleaned from a newspaper, as he stated during his first police interrogation, and did not require his director's say-so. Nor did the defendant require his director to point out to him in Munich that he could approach the Führer by means of a letter of recommendation. For, according to statements by Professors Ehrenspeck and Reuther, they had already discussed this possibility of gaining entrée to the Führer in Berchtesgaden.

If the defendant's testimony about the personality of his alleged director is practically unbelievable, and in part — as it pertains to the declaration of protection — even refuted, then there exists a high degree of probability, as stated in the expert testimony of Dr. Mayer, that the defendant committed the act of his own free will and without knowledge of other persons. He then invented the story about his director and their collaboration after his arrest so as to camouflage his true motives during the interrogations. After several sessions which Dr. Mayer conducted according to the so-called method of free association, whose nature and technique Dr. Mayer will further elaborate during the main hearing, he reached the conclusion that the defendant, as a strict Catholic and after several years of training in a seminary, regarded National Socialism as a danger to Catholicism. He performed his act as a religious fanatic and in the belief of his misunderstood mysticism and his calling as a martyr, and thought that the alleged danger could be removed by killing the Führer, not that these circumstances should in any way be regarded as diminishing his responsibility for his actions or eliminating them in any way.

The defendant's complete responsibility for his actions also follows from the thorough assessment by University Professor Dr. Müller-Haas who, after a thorough investigation of the defendant's state of mind, reached the conclusion that no doubts exist as to the defendant's sense of responsibility at the time of his deed.

If the defendant, as he claims, actually offered to kill the Führer and thereupon met with his alleged director to discuss the deed, he already committed an infraction of § 5 No. 1 of the Decree for the Protection of the People and the State of February 28, 1933. Above and beyond that, the defendant at the very least performed the attempts to execute the deed, which constitutes an undertaking to kill. One must already regard as attempted acts those which in their entirety represent immediately aggressive acts against the legally protected object, so that the endangerment of this legally protected object and the objective probability of fulfilling the intended act exists. (RGSt. Bd. 53 S. 217 and 336) The acquisition of the pistol, the defendant's practice shooting in Berchtesgaden, on the Ammensee and in the woods near Pasing, the acquisition of the grandstand ticket, the creation of the forged letters should only be regarded as preparatory acts. However, the defendant's actions immediately prior to an assassination attempt; that is, taking his seat on the grandstand with a loaded pistol in his pocket in anticipation of an opportune moment to shoot, the use of the forged letter of recommendations at the Schiessstätt Bridge at the Obersalzberg, and at the "Braune Haus" and "Haus des Führers" so as to gain entry to the Führer to shoot him then with the loaded pistol all constitute attempted acts and therewith fulfill the provisions of the undertaking to kill the Führer in the sense of § 5. No. 1 of the Decree for the Protection of the People and the State of February 28, 1933. The previously enumerated individual attempted acts by the defendant, since they resulted from a single on-going intention, constitute a continuous crime since they were directed against the same sanctity of the law and the life of the Führer and Reich Chancellor.

Proof

I   The Defendant's *Answers*:
Volume I Sheet 9/12, 63/81,
Volume II Sheet 11/17, 21/38, 45/63,
Volume III Sheet 1/21;

II   the *Witnesses*:
1) Kriminalsekretär Freiländer:
Supplement Sheet 1/59
2) Kriminaloberassistent Berchtenbreiter
Supplement Sheet 1/59
3) Landsgerichtsrat Waller in Berlin NW. 40, Turmstrasse 91:
Volume II Sheet 87/88, 141, 182, 187
Volume II Sheet 47
4) Salesgirl Paula Gutterer in Baden-Baden, Balzenbergstrasse 14:
Volume II Sheet 115/122
5) The married woman Karoline Gutterer née Nofaier in Baden-Baden, Balzenbergstrasse 14:
Volume II Sheet 123/129

6) Foreman Karl Gutterer in Baden-Oos, Zinzheimer-strasse 36:
   Volume II Sheet 133

7) Ministerial Director Leopold Gutterer in Berlin-Charlottenburg, Kaiserdamm 8:
   Volume III Sheet 42/43

8) The married woman Auguste Gutterer née Heil in Berlin-Charlottenburg, Kaiserdamm 8:
   Volume III Sheet 43/46

9) Postal Assistant Emil Merkel in Baden-Baden, Kapellmattstrasse 43:
   Volume II Sheet 135/136

10) Postal Assistant Josef Meier in Baden-Oos, Sternstrasse 5:
    Volume II Sheet 136/137

11) Pensioner Anna Radke née Schmidt in Berlin-Wilmersdorf, Berlinerstrasse 146:
    Volume II Sheet 188

12) Professor Willy Ehrenspeck in Berchtesgaden, High School:
    Volume II Sheet 67/71

13) Professor Emil Reuther in Berchtesgaden, High School:
    Volume II Sheet 73/76

14) Weapons dealer Hans Abele in Munich, Am Bergsteig 5:
    Volume II Sheet 160/162

15) Manager Emil Senftinger in Munich, Marsstrasse 12 III:
    Volume II Sheet 149/151

16) Newspaper reporter Albert Bintz in Munich, Rabelstrasse 25:
    Volume II Sheet 156/160

17) SS-Hauptsturmführer Karl Koch in Munich, Zech-
strasse 8 II:
Volume II Sheet 146/148
18) Office employee Irma Hill in Munich, Ainmiller
Strasse 1 IV:
Volume II Sheet 152/155
19) Landgerichtdirektor Dr. Kurt Hanssen in Munich, Ar-
mira-Platz 3 I:
Volume II Sheet 152/155

III the *Experts*
1) Kriminalsekretär Wolter of the Reich Criminal Police
Office in Berlin as authority on the expert opinion by
the Reich Handwriting Collection: Supplementary Volume Envelope 9
2) Handwriting expert Dr. Jeserich in Berlin-Charlotten-
berg, Fasanenstrasse 12, as authority on the expert
opinion: Volume II Sheet 205/213
3) Medical specialist Dr. Mayer in Heidelberg, Bienen-
strasse 1, as authority on the expert opinion in Volume
III Sheet 98/110

IV the following *documents* and other *pieces of evidence*:
1) the defendant's criminal record: File I, Envelope Ia
2) the defendant's passport:
Supplementary File, Envelope 1
3) the forged letter of recommendation, the camouflaged
letter for the Führer, and the declaration of protection:
Supplementary File, Envelope 2
4) the photo of Marcel Gerbohay with the defendant's dedication: Supplementary File, Envelope 2
5) the notification by Ministerial Director Gutterer to the
Gestapo:
Supplementary File, Envelope 3

6) photo copy of the police registry form of October 21, 1938
(Hotel Alexandra in Berlin): Supplementary File, Envelope 4

7) the receipt for the rented typewriter: Supplementary File, Envelope 5

8) the index of the contents in the bag the defendant left behind in Munich: Supplementary File, Envelope 7

9) the city plan of Munich and the map of the area surrounding Berchtesgaden: Supplementary File, Envelope 7

10) the accusatory beginning of the essay on the Jews: Supplementary File 8

11) the journal *Weltdienst*: File II, Envelope 5a

12) the photographic enlargement of the signature on the declaration of protection: Supplementary File, Envelope 9

13) the defendant's letter to the journal *Weltdienst* of October 2, 1938: Supplementary File, Envelope 11

14) the defendant's letter of credit: Supplementary File, Envelope 12

15) the torn-up pieces of paper the defendant left behind in the furnished room in Berlin: Supplementary File, Envelope 13

16) the married woman Karoline Gutterer's note about the place of origin of Marcel Gerbohay's letter: Supplementary File, Envelope 14

17) the police registry form of October 31, 1938 (Hotel Stadt Wien in Munich): Supplementary File, Envelope 15

18) the sheet which the pensioner Radke used to communicate with the defendant: Supplementary File, Envelope 16

19) the map of Baden-Baden: Supplementary File, Envelope 17

20) the autobiography which the defendant wrote himself: Supplementary File, Envelope 18

21) the four sets of comparison for the expert opinion of the handwriting expert Dr. Jeserich: Supplementary File, Envelope 19

22) the photo copy of the city map of Neuchâtel: Supplementary File, Envelope 20

23) the plan of the festivities of November 8 and 9, 1938: Supplementary File, Envelope 21

24) The books *Mein Kampf* and *Ma Doctrine* which the defendant left behind in the apartment of pensioner Radke, in a special package

25) the Schmeisser pistol with bullets and cleaning equipment, in a special package

V The *Files* Cs 1729/38 of the District Court in Augsburg

I move to order the trial of the defendant Maurice Bavaud before the 2nd Senate of the People's Court, to terminate the investigative detention, and to appoint a defense attorney for the defendant.

Lautz

Copy
II J 149/39 g
2 H 59/39

Secret!

In the Name
of the German People
In the Criminal Case against the technical draftsman Maurice *Bavaud*, born on January 15, 1916, in Neuchâtel (Switzerland), and still residing there, presently under investigative detention,

because of crimes against the Decree of February 28, 1933, the People's Court, 2nd Senate, in a public hearing on December 18, 1939, has, on the basis of oral arguments in which participated as judges:

Vice-president of the People's Court Engert, Chairman

People's Court Counselor Dr. Albrecht

SS-Brigadeführer Colonel of the Regular Police von Grolman

Reichsamssleiter Berkenkamp

Oberregierungsrat Dr. Taubert

as representatives of the Reich Attorney's Office:

Reich Attorney Weyersberg

as documentary official of the register office:

Legal secretary Koenitz

the court rules

that the defendant Bavaud, because of crimes against § 5 No. 1 of the the Reich President's Decree for the Protection of the People and the State of February 28, 1933 (RGB1. I S 83) is condemned to death and to pay the costs of the trial.

So justice be done.

Reasons.

At the trial which, since the defendant does not appear to have command of German, was conducted with the help of a translator from the French, the following determinations were made on the basis of the defendant's admissions:

I

The Personal Situation of the Defendant

The defendant is the oldest son of a mail carrier in Neuchâtel (Switzerland) and is a Swiss national. Both parents of the defendant are strict Catholics; especially the mother is anti-German.

The defendant attended grade school in Neuchâtel from age six to fourteen, briefly afterward the secondary school in the same town, and subsequently the technical school in Freiburg (Switzerland). In secondary school his grades were good, in technical school, however, less so. Around May 1932 he began an apprenticeship as a draftsman at the Favag Firm, a factory for electrical apparatuses in Neuchâtel, and after completing his schooling was also employed there for two months as a technical draftsman. During his student days he joined the St. Josef Association, which included youths between the ages of 16 and 25, which was then led by a vicar, and which, beside religious exercises, was devoted to sports and social games.

In winter 1934/5 the defendant also became a member of the Neuchâtel chapter of the Front National, which allegedly expressed anti-Semitic and anti-democratic as well as Swiss nationalist attitudes. After six or seven months the defendant left this above-mentioned party, first of all because he had a falling out with the local leadership, second because he disapproved of the pan-Germanic stance of the majority of the members of this political organization. During this time he also read a book which described the life of a missionary in the Congo and he decided to become a missionary himself. He conveyed this wish to the "Congregation de Saint Esprit," whose address was provided in the same book, and soon thereafter met one of its priests. During the interview he had to provide this priest with identification and information about himself and his family. After further negotiations at the missionary society's bureau in Freiburg (Switzerland), he was informed after a brief test that he would be sent to attend the seminary in St. Brieuc (Bretagne). The missionary society expressed its willingness to assume the major share of his educational costs, so that his parents only needed to contribute the boarding fee of approximately 100

Swiss francs a year. The training in the missionary profession was to take four years. Afterward, as a member of the society, he was to receive a seven-year education, in the sixth year of which he would have become a priest. The defendant began his preparatory education at the seminary in October 1935 and remained there, with the exception of vacations, until July 1938, when he went to Neuchâtel to spend the holidays with his parents. From this vacation he did not return to the seminary because, as he testified at the main hearing, he even then had the intention of traveling to Germany to perform the deed for which he is being held responsible at present.

However, he first tried to find a position in the profession of technical draftsman he had learned in Switzerland, and when he did not succeed he took a job in his mother's greengrocer shop in Neuchâtel. Beside free board and room he received from her the monthly salary of 50 francs. The defendant allegedly made no further contact with the Swiss party "Front National" after his return from St. Brieuc. Beside working in his mother's shop the defendant busied himself trying to learn German and Russian. However, he allegedly lacks sufficient command of German to express himself comprehensively.

II
The Facts of the Case

After his return from St. Brieuc the defendant preoccupied himself intensively with the atrocity stories in the more or less anti-German, especially Jewish-dominated Swiss press and also tended to lend credence to similar oral reports from members of Catholic orders, among others the Benedictines, who had emigrated from Germany. This decisively influenced the decision he had already been reached in St. Brieuc, to eliminate the German Führer and Chancellor who in his opinion was an enemy of Christianity and of humanity. So as to improve his chances of realizing this objective — or, to use the defendant's chief expression during the trial — "to achieve a better result," he decided first to familiarize himself with the thinking of National Socialism, so as to be able to pass himself off in Germany as a convinced adherent of this movement and, as he hoped, to be able to get closer to the Führer at the right time. Therefore he bought a French edition of *Mein Kampf* and the French collection of the Führer's most important speeches, which bears the title *Ma Doctrine*. On October 2, 1938, he also ordered a six-month subscription to the journal *Weltdienst*, and immediately sent the publisher a postal money order in the amount of 6 RM.

Moreover, at the beginning of October he now decided to translate his plan to kill the Führer into action and to take a trip to Germany for this purpose. Therefore on October 4, 1938, he had his passport extended to November 4, 1938, and provided himself with the necessary funds for his trip on the night of October 9, 1938, by obtaining a second key to his mother's safe in her store and taking 600 Swiss francs from it. The next day, Sunday October 9, 1938, between 6 and 7 A.M. he then drove from Neuchâtel to Basel, where upon his arrival he bought with the 538.35 francs in his possession a letter of credit in the amount of 555 RM at the exchange booth of the Dresdner Bank, and then continued his trip to Baden-Baden where he arrived at 2 P.M. Immediately after his arrival he went to the apartment of his great aunt, Mrs. Karoline Gutterer, whom he met in the company of her husband. He introduced himself as the grandson of her sister, and explained that he was in Germany for the express purpose of looking for work in his profession as a technical draftsman. On the day of the defendant's arrival the Gutterers happened to be visited by their nephew, the foreman Karl Gutterer, who knew French and with whom the defendant struck up a conversation about the political conditions during which he represented himself as an enthusiastic adherent of National Socialism and as an admirer of the Führer, so that his relatives had no apprehensions about helping him to find a job in Germany. So as to assist him in this endeavor, the stepdaughter of the Gutterers, the salesgirl Paula Gutterer, after first checking with the employment office in Baden-Baden, traveled with the defendant to Rastatt, taking along his vita, which she had noted down from his comments. In Rastatt they first looked up an official of the employment office with whom Paula Gutterer was acquainted, and who immediately sought to help the defendant by calling various firms. However, all attempts to find him a job remained unsuccessful.

The defendant stayed with his relatives in Baden-Baden until October 20, 1938, and spent most of his time walking around the city and its surroundings, at times in company of the child of the wife of the Departmental Director Gutterer in Berlin, who is a son of the Gutterers in Baden-Baden. So as to defray his personal expenses the defendant went several times to the Dresdner Bank branch in Baden-Baden and drew sums against his letter of credit. His relatives, who were aware that the defendant's parents were strict Catholics, noticed that he showed little interest in attending church on Sundays.

From Baden-Baden the defendant wrote his parents that he was staying with his relatives there, and also admitted to them that he had stolen the money from the safe, simultaneously asking them not to tell the relatives about this, so as not to bring him into ill repute.

On October 20, 1938, the defendant explained to his relatives that he would go to Mannheim to see if the Swiss consulate there could be instrumental in helping him find a job. He knew how to arrange it so that his relatives would not accompany him to the railroad station. There he first put his luggage on a train to the Anhalter railroad station in Berlin before himself taking the train to Basel where, for the price of 30 Swiss francs, he bought a pistol (Schmeisser, 6.35mm) from gunsmith Bürgin, Am Steinentor 13. Thereupon he began his trip to Berlin where he arrived sometime on October 21, 1938.

In Berlin the defendant first took a room in the hotel Alexandra in the Mittelstrasse and immediately registered with the police, using his correct name on an appropriately filled-out form. The morning of the next day he went to look for a furnished room, which he then found on the Berliner Strasse 146 in Wilmersdorf with the pensioner Anna Radke. To her question what his job was he replied traveling salesman. He immediately agreed to pay the monthly rent of 35 RM, and paid her 13 RM for the remaining days of October, and 2 RM for lighting costs. The defendant then bought 25 more bullets, caliber 6.35mm, in central Berlin, probably at the weapons shop on Friedrichstrasse, which were handed to him without further questions since there are no restrictions for the buying of ammunition for persons over the age of 18. The defendant then went with his luggage to Frau Radke's apartment where the latter called his immediate attention to the fact that he would have to register with the police and where, from the balcony of her apartment, she pointed out the location of the local police precinct. The defendant promised to take care of the matter and also to provide himself with the appropriate forms, which he filled out. On this or the next day the defendant read in the Paris newspaper *Le Jour* that, contrary to his expectation, the Führer was not in Berlin but in Berchtesgaden; therefore he decided to go there at once, to execute his murder plan. He told his landlady, whom he encountered the morning of his departure in the apartment hallway, that he would be going to Dresden for five days, and promised once more to register with the police. The defendant left the front door key with Frau Radke while keeping the apartment keys, contrary to Frau Radke's wishes, even though he had decided not to return to Berlin. Later he threw these keys, because they were worthless to him, into a trash can on a street in Munich. After the defendant had left the apartment, Frau Radke noticed that he had left a number of torn pieces of paper behind, which, however, according to Gestapo investigation, are not or are only loosely connected to the defendant's action. Furthermore, the defendant left a number of used clothing and toilet articles behind in his rented room, as well as several books, among them the French editions of *Ma Doctrine* and *Mein Kampf* as well as French-language textbooks.

After the defendant had changed the remaining 305 RM of his letter of credit into currency he went to the Anhalter railroad station and took the train to Berchtesgaden, where he arrived on October 25, 1938, took a room in the hotel Stiftskeller, and stayed there until October 31, 1938. During this time he took several walks in the surrounding area and used them to practice shooting his pistol. To this purpose he took approximately 25 shots at distances from between 7 and 8 meters at trees in the forest. Further, he once sought to gain entry to the Berghof, and therefore asked a policeman on the street in Berchtesgaden how one might approach it. However, the official explained to him that it was impossible to reach the vicinity of the Berghof on the Obersalzberg without passing through the blockade. At the suggestion of the manager of the hotel Stiftskeller the defendant looked up a professor Ehrenspeck during school hours at the high school in Berchtesgaden and after being introduced to him explained that because of his poor knowledge of German he sought the company of French-speaking persons in Berchtesgaden. Subsequently the aforementioned Professor Ehrenspeck and Professor Reuther, whom Ehrenspeck had brought along, met repeatedly with the defendant in different restaurants in Berchtesgaden. During his conversations with the two professors, the defendant repeatedly represented himself as a friend and admirer of National Socialist Germany and of the Führer, and also expressed the wish to meet and speak to the Führer, adding that this was the very purpose of his visit to Berchtesgaden. The two professors explained to him that it was scarcely feasible to speak to the Führer, but that it was to be expected that he would be present during the festivities in Munich on November 8 and 9, during which the defendant could see him. In this connection Ehrenspeck also mentioned to the defendant that years ago he had gotten the best view of the Führer during the memorial procession of November 9 by staying inside the Café City, where the street is very narrow, and stepping out of the café onto the street only at the moment the procession arrived. He further mentioned that an introduction to the Führer was probably only possible if the defendant could present a letter of recommendation from an influential personality.

On the basis of the information he had gathered from the two Berchtesgaden professors the defendant took the train to Munich on October 31, 1938 and took lodgings at the hotel Stadt Wien. He tried at several offices — that at City Hall, the Foreign Press Bureau, and the Feldherrnhalle — to obtain a ticket for a grandstand seat for the memorial procession on November 9, 1938, but was turned away everywhere with the remark that no further tickets were available. One of these offices, it is supposed to have been the one at City Hall, called the defendant's attention to the fact that he might still be able to obtain a grandstand seat at the Official Bureau for November 9, and so the defendant went there and indeed obtained a ticket simply by saying that he wanted to see the memorial procession out of sympathy for National Socialism, and was not asked to show an I.D. or explain the purpose of his visit to Munich. The following day, probably November 5, 1938, the defendant bought himself two packs of 6.35mm bullets at the weapons shop of weapon dealer Abele in Munich and several practice targets, as well as a third pack of bullets at a weapons store whose identity can no longer be determined. On the evening of November 5, 1938, the defendant happened to meet Professor Reuther on the Karlsplatz, whom he told that he had been lucky enough to obtain a grandstand seat for November 9.

On Sunday November 6, 1938, the defendant drove to Lake Ammensee, rented a rowboat, and rowed out onto the lake where he prepared little paper ships at which he fired from distances of between 4 to 6 meters so as to get further target practice. On one of the next days, probably on November 7, 1938, he went for the same purpose to Pasing, attached the practice targets he had bought in Munich to several trees, and continued to familiarize himself with the pistol. He claims that he took altogether approximately 80 practice shots at Lake Ammensee and in the woods near Pasing. After he returned to Munich he bought himself a plan of the festivities on November 8 and 9 from a street vendor and inscribed the course of the projected memorial march onto the Munich city plan which he had bought earlier. He then walked through the streets through which the march was to take place to ascertain the best spots from which to execute his intended act, and reached the conclusion that the Café City was the most opportune location because the street was narrowest there. At that point he even considered climbing on a chair or table and shooting through the window during the march, but he dismissed this plan soon afterwards because he regarded the distance as too great for a successful shot, and the grandstand also seemed more propitious to him!

On the morning of November 9, 1938, the defendant went so early to the grandstand opposite the Heiliggeist Church so as to get a seat in the first row, carrying the loaded pistol in his coat pocket with the intention of shooting the Führer if he could count on a high probability of hitting him. However, in the event that the distance proved too great he planned — since his seat was close to the entrance to the grandstand — to leave the grandstand, run toward the procession from that entrance, so as to get closer to the Führer, and shoot him. When the memorial procession approached, the defendant had to admit to himself that the distance between his grandstand seat and the spot where the Führer was marching among his companions was too great for a successful shot, and that he might conceivably hit one of the Führer's companions instead. However, since the defendant was solely interested in killing the Führer, and did not want to injure anyone else, something which might lead to his arrest, thus making the further pursuit of his plan impossible, and since the two rows of SA men prevented him from leaving the grandstand and getting closer to the Führer, he was unable to realize his objective. He therefore let the entire procession move past and then left the grandstand.

After he returned to his hotel the defendant remembered his conversation with the two professors in Berchtesgaden and formed the plan to try to gain entrée to the Führer by means of a forged letter of recommendation from former French president Flandin and to committ the assassination then. Therefore he prepared a handwritten alleged letter of recommendation by the above-mentioned French statesman and also forged his signature. He mentioned in this letter that the bearer, Maurice Bavaud, had to hand the letter over personally to the Führer, and placed the forgery into an envelope. So as to be safe in case he would be asked for the letter before gaining admission to the Führer, he prepared yet a second letter by putting a blank sheet of paper into an envelope, sealing it, and writing the words Reich Chancellor on the envelope. The defendant traveled with these letters on November 10, 1938, at noon from Munich to Berchtesgaden where he arrived between 5 and 6 P.M. He immediately took a taxi to the Obersalzberg, at the bottom of which he was stopped by a police guard at the Schiessstätt Bridge.

After being asked about his business, the defendant replied that he came from Paris to give a letter to the Führer. When he was informed that the Führer was not on the Obersalzberg, the defendant took the same taxi straight back to the railroad station and the same evening took the train back to Munich. The defendant now wanted to try to be personally received by the Führer in Munich which made him reflect that a handwritten letter of recommendation might arouse suspicion and it might be better to type the letter as well as the addresses on the envelopes. On November 11, 1938, he therefore rented a typewriter for two days and had it brought to his hotel the same day. The defendant now wrote a new letter of recommendation on this typewriter in which he however changed the person who recommended him into the French National Assembly delegate Pierre Taittinger, whose signature he also forged. Defendant did this because he could not exclude the possibility that the signature of the former French president Flandin might be known to the Führer or persons in his circle and that the forgery might thus be revealed at once. The defendant also forged the addresses on the envelopes with the typewriter. The letter in question went like this:

Paris 10 octobre 1938

Excellence

Ayez l'obligeance, je vous prie, de bien vouloir recevoir Monsieur Maurice Bavaud. Je lui ai confié un pli qu'il ne vous remettra qu'en main propre. Il s'agit d'une communication essentiellement privée, bien qu'il soit question de politique.

Veuillez agréer, Excellence, l'assurance de toute ma considération.

Pierre Taittinger.
Député de Paris & président du parti Rép.
National & Soc.

This letter reads in translation:

Your Excellency,
I ask you to be so kind as to receive Mr. Maurice Bavaud. I have entrusted a letter to him which he will hand only to you personally. It is primarily a private matter, though it also touches on politics.

Your Excellency, please be assured of my highest respect.

Pierre Taittinger
Delegate from Paris and
President of the Rep. National
Soc. Party.

The defendant typed the words "Reich Chancellor" on the open envelope which contained this letter, and on the closed envelope, which merely contained a blank sheet of paper: "Monsier le Chancelier Adolf Hitler (aux bons soins de M. M. Bavaud)."

On the morning of November 12, 1938, the defendant went with these forged documents and the loaded pistol to the "Braune Haus" in Munich at whose entrance he was asked by the guard SS-Hauptsturmführer Koch what his business was, whereupon defendant showed the forged letter of recommendation to the guard and replied that he had to deliver the letter personally to the Führer. During these negotiations Koch called upon an employee who knew French who then served as the translator. Guard Koch telephoned the appropriate expert in Reichsleiter Bormann's office, Landgerichtsdirektor Dr. Hanssen, and conveyed the defendant's wish as well as the content of the letter to him. The defendant thereupon was led to Dr. Hanssen who, however, explained to him that a personal audience with the Führer out of the question for the defendant. After the defendant continued to insist that he had to hand over the letter personally to the Führer, Dr. Hanssen suggested to him either to send it by mail or give it to him, Dr. Hanssen, who would make sure that the letter would reach the Führer's hand. When the defendant also rejected these suggestions and continued to insist on a personal audience with the Führer, Dr. Hanssen urged him to call on the Reich Chancellory, whereupon the defendant left the "Haus des Führers" and, around noon the same day, took the train to Bischofswiesen where he arrived between 4 and 6 P.M. Since all he had left were 5 RM, defendant proposed to walk to the Reich Chancellory on foot and also asked several persons whom he met on the way for directions. However, since it had become dark in the meantime and it had also occurred to him that offices generally closed earlier on Saturday afternoons, the defendant gave up his planned visit to the Reich Chancellory as unpromising and returned to the Bischofswiesen railroad station. So as not to run out of funds completely, the defendant bought himself a ticket only as far as Freilassing, and then mounted the Berchtesgaden train to Munich. In Freilassing the wagons of the Berchtesgaden train had been attached to the Munich–Stuttgart–Karlsruhe–Paris express, and so the defendant transferred to the Paris express wagons at the front of the train in Munich. When the trip continued the defendant was asked for his ticket by a conductor, and when he replied that he had lost it he was asked to buy a new one, at which point his impecuniousness became evident. Therefore the defendant was handed over to the railroad police at the next stop, which was Augsburg, who then, because he was a foreigner, handed him on to the Gestapo.

Upon his arrest, the Gestapo found on his person, aside from his passport, the forged letter of recommendation with the forged signature of Pierre Taittinger, as well as the envelope meant for the Führer, money in the amount of 1.52 RM, the Schmeisser pistol, whose magazine was still loaded with six bullets, as well as an envelope with a note with the following text written on it:

"*Cet homme est sous ma protektion immediate et n'a rien fait qui ne soit selon mes ordres.*"

Which in translation says:

"This man stands under my immediate protection and has done nothing which does not conform to my orders."

Beneath this text were three intertwined letters which evidently represent an *A*, an *H*, and a *B*, with a line drawn through them.

After his arrest on November 24, 1938, the defendant was taken to the court in Augsburg, which issued an arrest warrant for him for the illegal possession of arms and for ticket fraud, and which then sentenced him to two months and one week in prison for these misdemeanors. Of this sentence the one week which the defendant spent in investigative detention was forgiven, and the remainder was served from December 14, 1938, to February 14, 1939

III
The Indictment and the Defendant's Response

On the basis of these facts the defendant is accused in the indictment of having continuously undertaken to kill the Führer and Reich Chancellor in October and November 1938 in Baden-Baden, Berlin, Berchtesgaden, Munich and Bischofswiesen, which is a crime against § 5 No. 1 of the Decree of the Reich President for the Protection of the People and the State of February 28, 1933 (RGBI. I S. 83).

In the course of all these proceedings and also during the trial the defendant frankly admitted that he had the serious intention of killing the German Führer and Reich Chancellor and that this had been the sole purpose for his coming to Germany, and also for his visits to Berlin, Berchtesgaden and Munich.

Despite proof to the contrary, he stubbornly insisted throughout the judicial inquiry that he committed his crime only on the order of a highly placed German personality, whom he had met in Neuchâtel in the summer of 1938 upon his return from St. Brieuc, and with whom he met repeatedly during his stay in Germany, in Baden-Baden, in Berlin and in Munich, sometimes also in company of his two companions. This personality, whom the defendant calls his "protector" and whose name he was never willing to divulge, wanted — so the defendant claimed during the investigative proceeding — the Führer removed because the Führer, though he had generously rebuilt the German army, did not wish to use it, out of his great love of peace, to realize certain pan-Germanic aims, and therefore blocked the political objectives of his "protector."

During the trial the defendant dropped all these mystifications and contrary to his previous answers allowed how he had prepared the note himself and that the director did not exist at all, but rather that he, the defendant, had come up with the criminal plan to kill the Führer all by himself. Asked about his motives at the trial, the defendant stated that, on the basis of what he had read in the Swiss press and had heard from members of Catholic orders who had emigrated from Germany, he regarded the person of the Führer and Reich Chancellor a danger to humanity, and primarily also to Switzerland, whose independence he threatened. But church reasons more than any other had been responsible for his actions; because the Catholic Church and Catholic organizations were being surpressed in Germany, he therefore believed that he was doing a service to humanity and to all of Christendom with his act. This intention of his had also been closely connected to his inner calling to be a missionary. However — so he stated in his final summary — "he exaggerated his own role" and now regretted his act.

In addition he provided the following details. Aside from wanting to visit his relatives in Baden-Baden he had also wanted to familiarize himself with conditions in Germany and gain insight into the National Socialist party. The fact that he stole money from his parents so as to be able to travel to Germany did not appear that reprehensible to him in view of his objective, and he could justify it to himself in view of his intention.

The defendant gave up his undertaking on November 12, 1938, in Bischofswiesen only because he had no more money. Otherwise he would have continued to wait for an opportune moment to commit his murderous assassination attempt.

IV
The Factual and Legal Assessment

The defendant's extensive confession *actually* proves that he traveled to Germany in on October 9, 1938, with the sole intention of killing the German Führer and Reich Chancellor, and then traveled on to Berlin, Berchtesgaden and Munich in the expectation of realizing his murderous plans there. Beside the defendant's confession, the Senate also sees unequivocal proof of this fact in that the defendant took extensive target practice in the area around Munich with a pistol he had bought for the above-mentioned purpose, so as to become highly proficient and accurate.

As far as the legal assessment of the confirmed behavior of the defendant is concerned, he has in at least two instances become guilty of the crimes with which he was charged by the prosecution; that is, by going to the grandstand opposite the Heiliggeist Church in Munich on November 9, 1938, while the procession of the memorial march with the Führer passed by; and second, by allowing himself to be led into the "Haus des Führers" on November 12, 1938, and trying there with all the lies and deception at his command to be admitted to the Führer. In both instances the defendant has admitted carrying a loaded pistol ready and within reach in his pocket, and also frankly admits that he would have used this weapon against the Führer if he had succeeded in getting close enough to him to be able to shoot. However, in neither case was the defendant able to put his plan into action since in both instances he was prevented by circumstances beyond his control and much to his dislike: on November 9, 1938, by the fact that the procession marched past on the side of the street opposite the grandstand and that therefore the distance from the defendant's grandstand seat to where the Führer was marching with his old comrades was far too great to allow an absolutely certain shot, and also because the double row of SS men at the grandstand prevented the defendant's alternate plan of leaving the grandstand and running toward the Führer from being carried out; and on November 12, 1938, the defendant's planned assassination was thwarted because, despite stubborn and devious efforts on his part, he was not admitted to the Führer. In both instances the defendant's planned crimes were not performed and completed but remained stuck in the attempt. But contrary to the position taken by the defense it became evident from the trial that the activity developed by the defendant in both instances not only bore the character of merely preparatory acts but also constituted the beginning of the performance of the crimes the defendant intended to commit according to § 5 No. 1 of the Decree of the Reich President for the Protection of the People and the State of February 28, 1933. For in both instances the mere presence of the defendant, who in his fanaticism was capable of anything, on the grandstand and in the "Haus des Führers" constituted an immediate threat to the life and health of the Führer. Regarding the events on November 9, 1938, this determination requires no further elaboration here. But also the defendant's mere presence in the "Haus des Führers" on November 12, 1938, represented an immediate threat to the person of the Führer because, no matter that one may feel that the defendant's attempts to meet the

Führer were futile from the very start, the possibility that the defendant might actually have accidentally encountered the Führer or come close enough to him on his way to or from the office of Dr. Hanssen to have the opportunity to execute his criminal intentions cannot be absolutely excluded.

In neither instance did there exist a willingness on the part of the defendant to desist from carrying out his plan in the sense of § 46 StGB; for in both cases, as described in detail above, he did not desist in the completion of his actions because of a decision arising from his own free will but admittedly only because circumstances independent of his will prevented him from performing his criminal attack on the Führer. Clear proof of this determination can also be found in the fact that the defendant three days after the failure of his criminal plan on November 9, 1938, sought energetically and deviously to be admitted to the "Haus des Führers." After the failure of this further attempt he traveled to Bischofswiesen to pursue a personal audience with the Führer.

Even if the defendant's behavior in both instances must be legally evaluated as the inception of the execution of his intended crime of killing the Führer, that is, as a punishable attempt, the Senate on the other hand believed, agreeing in this with the prosecutor, that the defendant's presence in Berlin and Berchtesgaden sufficed to find him guilty on the same counts. For the investigation does not provide the slightest proof that the defendant tried to approach the Führer also in Berlin, something which he himself strenuously denies. In his attempt in Berchtesgaden on November 10, 1938, to reach the Obersalzberg and the Berghof, he was turned away by the police guard at the Schiessstätt Bridge. Even if the Führer had been at the Berghof on that date and the defendant had succeeded in duping the guard, it could not be expected that the defendant would actually have come so close to the Führer as to pose an actual threat without first being examined more closely. Since no immediate threat to the Führer occurred and could not have occurred, the Senate did not feel that it could determine a punishable act with sufficient certainty.

The two proved criminal acts against § 5 No. 1 of the previously cited decree arose from a uniformly directed decision by the defendant. From the very beginning he was intent on total success. The two individual acts as part of the total activity of the defendant stand closely connected to each other in time and were directed against the same legally protected object, the life and health of the Führer and Reich Chancellor. Therefore there exists legally a uniform (continuous) action which, moreover, contains all the objective and subjective characteristics of an undertaking realized in trial form to commit a crime according to § 5 No. 1 of the Decree of the Reich President for the Protection of the People and the State of February 28, 1933.

Neither the defendant himself nor the defense cast any doubt on the defendant's accountability or sense of responsibility for his actions. On the contrary, the defendant's entire cautious, consistent and devious behavior during the execution of his plan, no less than the manner in which he responded during the investigative proceeding and during the trial to the weighty charges leveled against him, showed that we are dealing with an intellectually alert and intelligent person whose complete mental accountability and sense of responsibility is legally not in doubt.

German penal law applies to the defendant, who is a Swiss national, according to § 3 StGB.

Finally, it must be noted that the defendant was convicted at the trial

of having sought continuously to kill the Führer and Reich Chancellor in November 1938 in Munich — a crime according to § 5 No. 1 of the Decree of the Reich President for the Protection of the People and State of February 28, 1933 (RGBL. I S. 83).

V
Punishment

The aforementioned § 5 of the Decree of February 28, 1933, from which the punishment due to the defendant can be derived, left the Senate the choice among the death penalty, life imprisonment and temporary imprisonment. The only appropriate atonement for the ruthless act and its extraordinary severity and the unusual tenacity of the criminal intent as manifested in the defendant time and time again can only be the highest penalty, that of death.

The defendant may not have had a criminal record and may have been a relatively young and immature person. It may also be correct that he received a completely skewed and false picture of the conditions in the new Germany on account of the ghastly stories circulating in the entire Swiss press as well as those that are disseminated by the malicious hearsay of members of the Catholic orders who have emigrated from Germany; and this misinformation may have motivated the defendant's Catholic fanaticism to perpetrate his damnable act.

However, these facts in no way mitigate the defendant's actions; for, from the moment of his entry into the Reich (October 9, 1938) until his arrest (November 13, 1938) he had ample opportunity in various cities and towns in Germany to convince himself that the true conditions in National Socialist Germany are very different from those represented to him in the Jewish-influenced press abroad, especially in Switzerland, or as these conditions had been described to him by unconscionable and homeless liars. Nor should it have taken him long to convince himself that in the new Germany neither of the two great religions, least of all the Catholic Church, encounter the slightest difficulty in disseminating their beliefs and dogmas among their members, and this despite their fundamentally unfriendly attitude toward National Socialism; that no one is prevented from attending church in Germany or in the performance of religious exercises and that therefore there is not the slightest justification to speak of the suppression of Christianity in Germany. Nor could it have remained concealed from the defendant that in Germany — in contrast to other countries which are favored by the democracies — not a single church or monastery has been destroyed or closed, that not a single priest has been slaughtered or a single nun raped or a single martyr's grave desecrated; but rather, that the bells are tolling in every church in German lands where the faithful are being called to attend services. The defendant, therefore, as the strict Catholic that he is, had not the least occasion to regard the Führer as an enemy of Christendom and use this as the moral justification for his criminal intention.

Nor as a Swiss citizen did he have the least occasion to be intent on the removal of the Führer and Chancellor. When the Führer tenaciously and at the last minute saved his German people from the dire abyss of internal and external political, economic, social and spiritual ruin and racial disintegration, when he in restless, well-aimed reconstructive work led his people to the might and greatness which is commensurate to their great historical past and great cultural achievements; when the Führer united the German people, who had been fractured for centuries, into an inwardly and outwardly closed body of people, within the framework of the German Reich, then he has not harmed any other people in the world in the slightest or diminished their justified rights. In particular, he has never reached out for the German cantons in Switzerland, and neither he nor any other influential person of Nationalist Socialist Germany has done or said anything from which one could glean a pan-Germanic ambition directed, among others, also at Switzerland. On the contrary, the Führer, in front of the entire world, has repeatedly affirmed his constant respect for the independence and neutrality of Switzerland within its present borders. Thus there was not the slightest reason for a nationalistic motivation or provocation for a criminal attack on the life of the Führer.

On the other hand, the defendant took it upon himself to deprive the German people of their savior, of a man for whom eighty million German hearts beat in love, admiration and gratitude, and whose strength and firm leadership are more essential for his people today than at any other time; and the defendant has done all this without even the slightest moral justification, solely out of his religious-political fanaticism. It therefore seemed self-evident to the Senate that such gangster-like acts by political Catholicism could only be met by the highest, the death penalty.

Since the defendant as a Swiss national in Germany lacked all rights as a citizen and all titles, offices, decorations or other perquisites as described in §§ 33, 34 StGB, the Senate felt that there was no need to deprive the defendant of such rights, as the indictment had asked. The fact that his actions are especially heinous is already sufficiently recognized by the defendant's condemnation to the highest and heaviest penalty available under German penal law.

Since the court in Augsburg, on December 6, 1938, already seized the defendant's weapon, its further seizure according to § 40 StGB becomes superfluous.

The division of the court costs underlies § 465 StPo.

[signed] Engert   Dr. Albrecht

Since the Koblenz historian Oldenhage found Bavaud's files in the Foreign Office Archives the reaction of the "gentlemen" officiating in the Wilhelmstrasse is still partially discernible:

Ref: WLR. Dr. Siedler   re R 2597 g
                              Note.

The Swiss ambassador was already informed several days ago, after he had made an inquiry, that Bavaud was condemned to death.

                              Copies.

I. Bei Pol. I, Pol II Sz, im Ref. Dtschd, im Rev. Partai z. gfl. Kts.

2. Chef AO

3. Filed

                    Berlin, January 2, 1940

Note re St. S. No. 28

The verdict against Bavaud (R. 2597 g) is enclosed. M.E. finds the content suitable enough to confront the Swiss ambassador with it during his next visit. The plan to murder the Führer was prepared by the Swiss national Bavaud, a member of the Catholic seminary St. Brieuc, out of Catholic political opposition to National Socialist Germany, and was done with malice aforethought and every imaginable deviousness. What is especially noteworthy is, as the verdict notes, that the defendant's acts were motivated by what he read in Swiss newspapers.

                         MDgt. Pol.
                    State Undersecretary
                           to the
                      State Secretary

with the request to take notice.

                    Berlin, January 11, 1940.
                         [signature]

Press notified.

Handwritten addition:

Significant content of the verdict:
Made into an assassin by being "educated" at St. Brieuc Seminary (in Brittany).

St. S. No. 28   Berlin, January 9, 1940

The *Swiss* ambassador today mentioned to me a Swiss citizen by the name of Bavaud who has been sentenced to death because of an attempt on the Führer's life. The legal section of the Foreign Office informed the Swiss embassy about the matter and remarked at the same time that publication of this event was not desired. Herr Frölicher made no petition in the case but mentioned that of course it would be easier to keep the matter under wraps if there were no execution.

[signed] Weizsäcker

Herrn U. St. S. Legal Section
Herrn U. St. S. Political Section
Herrn Dg. Political Section
German Desk
Press

Apparently so as to deceive the Nazis and to win time, Bavaud occasionally mentioned Marcel Gerbohay, that fellow seminarian whom he still deemed safe in a France which had not yet been overrun by Hitler. But since Bavaud repeatedly and expressedly confessed that he had attempted to kill the tyrant entirely on his own, we do not need to print the indictment and verdict against the similarly beheaded Gerbohay: they are not part of Bavaud's life history. What remains incomprehensible is why the ingloriously unfortunate Gerbohay did not go into hiding when the Germans occupied France.

Two "Führer-informations" and one excerpt from a "situation report" by the Reich attorney general of October 3, 1940, regarding Bavaud, from the Federal Archive in Koblenz (R22/4089, Reichsjustizministerium, R 22/3390, R 22/4089).
Führer Information September 7, 1942
1) Adviser: Oberregierungsrat Dr. Hupperschwiller
The total number of death sentences presented with petitions for mercy in the month of July 1942 is 241 as compared to 233 in June 1942.
Of the verdicts:
46 are for murder, attempted murder and violent crimes,
114 for war crimes and acts by career criminals,
7 for arson,
51 for high treason,
23 for treason.
Furthermore, the special courts in the incorporated Eastern territories sent in 216 death sentences in July 1942. In these cases the Reichsstatthalter or the Oberpräsidenten decided on the petitions for mercy.

2) Adviser: Ministerialrat Dr. Dittrich.
The Swiss national Maurice Bavaud, who was executed on May 14, 1941, had planned to assassinate you, my Führer, in November 1938. He claimed that the French national Marcel *Gerbohay*, whom he considered to be the son of a Russian count, urged him to commit this act.
Gerbohay has now been apprehended in occupied France. At his interrogation in Paris he called himself the leader of the "Mysterious Union" which has made it its objective to kill you,

my Führer. Gerbohay admits having sent Bavaud to Germany to commit the assassination. His background in France is one of poverty and he used his alleged Russian origins only to gain a greater sway over his followers.

The Attorney General of the   Berlin W 9, October 3, 1942
Reich at the People's Court   Bellevuestr. 15
                                               Tel: 21 83 41
sign: 4206 e–2.33.
(Please use in your reply)

To
the Reich Minister of Justice
in
Berlin W 8,
Wilhelmstrasse 65.

Decree of October 25, 1935 — IIIa 19570.35.
Enclosed: 2 copies of situation reports.

Situation Report

A. High Treason

I. Marxist High Treason

1. Altreich

Conditions have remained essentially unchanged since the preliminary report of August 1, 1942. The investigations which have been undertaken in the meantime almost exclusively concern Marxist oral propaganda by individuals or by groups of only a few persons. Only the four following events are worth special mention:

a) In the proceeding 6 J 114/42 against Freund and Others, ten defendants, among them five Alsatian workers, have been arrested, who disseminated Communist oral propaganda and perpetrated or planned acts of sabotage. It becomes evident from the files that the majority of Frenchmen and Alsatians who work in Constance are dissatisfied with the present conditions and long for Germany's defeat. Many Alsatians hope in such an event for a "free and independent" Alsatia or for reunification with France. Other Alsatians, but also Frenchmen, are of a Communist persuasion and tend to engage in Communist plans for an overthrow of the government. The chief defendant, the turner Viktor Freund, has repeatedly committed factory sabotage by intentionally slowing down his work or by putting work material aside. He was able to persuade his codefendants, at times successfully, to engage in similar acts of sabotage. He acquired the material for his incitations by listening to enemy radio stations. He provided several of his codefendants with a Communist book. The codefendant Ballast, an Alsatian, committed sabotage in a similar manner and in July 1942 drove to Mühlhausen with yet another defendant to get French hand grenades for illegal purposes, which he had hidden there after the French had moved out.

b) The proceeding 5 J 130/42 against Duc and Others is directed against three youthful defendants who were still young when they committed their crime, and who belonged to an anti-German group of Alsatian and French workers in Constance. One of the accused was for a time a member of the Hitler Youth. Their treasonable activity consisted of publically attaching placards with a inflammatory anti-German content (Long live Roosevelt, Stalin and Churchill! Down with Germany! Long live France! etc).

c) The Frenchman Marcel Gerbohay, who wanted to become a priest and who had been prosecuted in the 6 J 116/42 proceeding in 1938 together with approximately ten other French seminarians, founded the "Compagnie du Mystere" whose only objective supposedly was to fight Communism. He has confessed that as the leader of this group he recruited the Swiss Maurice Bavaud in 1938 to travel to Germany and to have the Führer declare war on Russia, and if he did not succeed in this, to kill the Führer. (Bavaud indeed did travel to Germany in 1938 and was sentenced and executed for crimes against § 5 No. 1, 1933 by the People's Court.) A report about this case was already filed on September 12, 1942.

d) On May 18, 1942, Jewish criminals placed one explosive and one fire bomb in the exhibition "The Soviet Paradise" in the Lustgarten in Berlin, which was to set the exhibition on fire. The Jews who participated in this attack were condemned to death by a special court in Berlin and were executed.

The Reich Minister of Justice

Führer Information
1942 No. 131

On December 18, 1939, the People's Court condemned Maurice Bavaud, a Swiss national with strong Catholic ties — for a time he attended a Catholic monastery in Brittany — to death. In 1938 Bavaud was preparing to assassinate you, my Führer. Even at that time we could find traces among French clerical circles. Now the People's Court will try the Frenchman Marcel Gerbohay, who belonged to these circles and who incited Bavaud to perform this assassination attempt. Gerbohay has confessed.

Berlin, October 14, 1942

Copy No. 3

Engert, Vice-President of the People's Court, who signed the death sentence of December 18, 1939 together with Dr. Albrecht, the Court Counselor (this denunciation is a "reminder" for Bavaud's German defense attorney, who was more than just the "court-appointed laywer"), then accused the Berlin lawyer Wallau on January 5, 1940, after first checking and reaching an agreement with the "Chief of the Führer's Chancellory":

The Deputy President   Berlin W 9, January 5, 1940
of the People's Court   Bellevuestrasse 15

To
  The NS-Rechtswahrerbund
  attention of Herr Dr. Heuber
  in
  Berlin W 35
  Tiergartenstrasse 20

Dear Party Member Dr. Heuber!
  On December 18, 1939, the 2nd Senate of the People's Court under my chairmanship engaged in a proceeding $\frac{11\ J\ 149.39^a}{2\ H\ 59.39}$ against the Swiss national Maurice Bavaud because of a crime committed against the Decree of February 28, 1933 (assassination attempt on the Führer). The crime was prepared down to the smallest detail. We can only thank pure chance that it was not actually committed. From the point of view of justice there was never the slightest doubt that what came under consideration was a completed act, and not merely the preparation thereto.

  Nonetheless, Bavaud's defense attorney, the lawyer Dr. Franz *Wallau*, Berlin W 62, Landgrafstrasse 10, dared to ask for the acquittal of his client because he allegedly only engaged in preparatory acts.

  The request produced the greatest astonishment in the Chancellory of the Führer as well as among the members of the Senate. It is the nearly unanimous opinion of the Senate that a lawyer who misunderstands his duties as a defense attorney to such a degree has demonstrated that he is unfit for his profession.

Again in complete agreement with the Senate and with the Chief of the Führer's Chancellory I ask that you consider the expulsion of this "defense attorney."

Heil Hitler!

Engert

7. Those parts of Sir Noel Mason-MacFarlane's estate which are sufficiently harmless to be made available to the public can be found in the Imperial War Museum in London. During his lifetime — he died in 1953 — Sir Noel told *Who's Who* that his favorite activity was "writing," and informed his wife and his daughter and son-in-law, who in turn told this to the British historian David Irving, how much he regretted that what he had noted down from his exciting times as military attaché with Hitler and Stalin and later as governor of Gibraltar and British commander in chief in Italy could be printed only in the distant future. But these notes have in the meantime been sifted through, have disappeared, because Mason-MacFarlane was also the man who, as his host in Gibraltar, urgently warned the Polish president Sikorski not to climb aboard the airplane in which Sikorski was murdered a few minutes after the machine had rolled to the very tip of the runway.

David Irving can confirm that Sikorski's widow told him and Hochhuth twice, in the presence of witnesses, how Sir Noel, soon after Sikorski's death, came to her in London and told her, and with tears in his eyes, how hard he, Sir Noel, had sought to persuade the general and his daughter, who was murdered with him, not to climb aboard the plane. . . . The Scotsman added that, first of all, the great precautions the British had taken to guard the VIP-Liberator on the runway excluded the possibility that Germans could have approached the plane in which the Polish commander in chief and his staff were murdered; second, it was impossible that the Russians could have gotten to it; third, the landing of the Liberator not far from the coast, which he and his staff had observed, "could not have been an accident."

It is no surprise that nothing of this, nor of his trip to London to see Madame Sikorska, can be found in Mason-MacFarlane's estate.

The first of the two conversations which Madame Sikorska held with Irving and Hochhuth took place on June 26, 1966, in the apartment of Mr. and Mrs. Lisiewicz in South Kensington; Mr. Lisiewicz was a staff officer with Sikorski and was one of the Poles who accompanied their commander in chief on his trip to the Kremlin, the first of *four* successive flights of the president during which his plane, invariably a so-called VIP-machine furnished to him by Downing Street, had *five* "incidents" or "accidents." . . . The second conversation took place a few days later in the house of Madame Sikorska and her sister, who was also present.

During this second conversation Madame Sikorska handed Irving and Hochhuth two photos of a troop inspection undertaken by Churchill and Sikorski in Scotland, photos that had been selected from a series of ten or twelve that were taken on that occasion, incidentally before the rest were given to the Archive of the British Imperial War Museum.

Peter Hoffmann in his book *Die Sicherheit des Diktators* (Munich, 1975), reports that Mason-MacFarlane had long been of the opinion that Hitler's politics had to lead to war because the German dictator would not stop attacking and blackmailing one country after the other until the big powers put an end to it. Even Sir Nevile Henderson, who had long sympathized with the German government, after the occupation of Prague in March 1939 reached the conclusion that one could not trust Hitler, and that the politics of appeasement were not achieving their purpose. But the attaché was always a few steps ahead of the ambassador in his assessment of the situation, as the manager of the embassy, Sir George Ogilvie-Forbes, reports on March 29, 1939 to Mr. Strang in Whitehall: "The military attaché is in a very warlike mood and wishes that we declare war on Germany in three weeks! It has been confidentially suggested to him that he should first put his thoughts in writing." Mason-MacFarlane did that and suggested immediately starting a war on two fronts against Germany, as long as the chances for victory were still good. Since the Foreign Office did not want to entertain his notions, the attaché delivered a different suggestion in person, as he reported in 1951: "I urgently advised London to murder Hitler. My Berlin apartment was less than 100 meters from the Führer's grandstand during the parades. All that one needed was a good rifleman and a H.V. rifle with telescope and silencer. One would have been able to shoot from a spot 10 meters behind my open bathroom window. The music and the other noise would have completely drowned out the little bang, so that no one could have determined where the shot came from." But London did not find the military attaché's suggestion acceptable.

8. Ernst Jünger: *Jahre der Okkuptation* (Stuttgart, 1958). On June 15, 1945, Jünger noted in Kirchhorst: "Visitors from the immense army of Germans that is flooding along the highways. . . . Yesterday Martin von Katte stopped by and stayed overnight. . . . We happened to talk about the 20th of July and von Stauffenberg. Rommel said as he drove off: 'Didn't someone have a captain with an army pistol?' The fact that the colonel had only one hand and that he was indispensable in the Bendlerstrasse may explain why he used a bomb. . . . Assassinations are sham solutions, just like suicides; they push the problems onto another, not a better level. . . ."

Jünger, who in this diary also provides a commentary of his reading of the Old Testament, speaks frequently of assassinations if only for that reason; however, he fails to consider whether a field marshal who on June 17, 1944, during a conversation with Hitler in France, 200 kilometers behind the invasion front — in a small circle that consisted solely of his and Hitler's adjudant Schmundt as well as Field Marshal von Rundstead and his adjudant, where he had to withdraw into an airraid bunker — was even *permitted* to ask the question whether "one didn't have a captain with an army pistol." Rommel himself, like all officers, of course carried a pistol during this dramatic confrontation with the dictator! Just as much as on June 29 at Hitler's Berghof when Rommel saw him for the last time and presented him with such a drastic clarification of the hopelessness of the German military situation in France that Hitler left the room during Rommel's lecture without even saying goodbye.

9. *Hitlers Tischgespäche in Führerhauptquartier* 1941–42, collected by DR. Henry Picker, newly edited by Percy Ernst Schramm (Stuttgart: Seewald Verlag, 1963).

Hitler is here speaking mistakenly of 1937 unless the SA-Standartenführer Dr. Werner Koeppen, Alfred Rosenberg's liaison officer at the Führer's headquarters, who transcribed this table talk, misheard.

Report Nr. 28.
Führerhauptquartier, Sunday, September 7, 1941
Lunch, September 6.
Guests: none
. . . The Führer happened to speak about assassination attempts against him and recounted by what luck he had escaped certain death. Especially a Swiss waiter had laid in wait for him

a long time in 1937. He managed to obtain an honorary ticket on November 1, 1937 for the grandstand but had never gotten a shot off since the hands raised to greet him prevented the assassin from having an accurate target. He was arrested by accident later on a train. The Führer was speculating whether one should even hold the November 9 procession. The entire leadership of the Reich was together during a long march through narrow and blind streets. The greatest danger for him of course was during the Reich Party Day, but there was no avoiding that really. The fact that he was spared by the explosive device set off in the Bürgerbräukeller on November 9, 1939 was entirely due to the circumstance that he could not use the plane because of the bad weather, and therefore had to leave somewhat sooner on the special train.

Indeed, already in the following year, in 1939, Hitler no longer dared, as he did never again, but as he had always until then, to repeat the "memorial procession of 1923" in company of his faithful to the Feldherrnhalle. . . . On May 3, 1942, he said during lunch at his table, speaking again about Bavaud — as always without mentioning his name — that "the only thing to do temporarily was to live an irregular life and to take one's walks, excursions and travels completely irregularly. . . . Therefore, whenever he decided to go somewhere he would leave all of a sudden, without even notifying the police. He even gave the strictest orders to the head of his security detail, Rattenhuber, and his chauffeur Kempka to keep his trips an absolute secret, and had pointed out to them that they had to obey this order no matter how high-placed an authority asked them for information.

"Because as soon as, say, the police knew that he would be going on a trip, they stopped their usual way of doing business and by this fact alone alarmed the population, without being aware that anything that breaks the rules is noticed."

10. The author wishes to express his thanks to Herr Director Dr. Beat Dumont and his teacher in Basel, Herr Professor Dr. Edgar Bonjour, to whom he was recommended once more by Herr Dr. Fredy Gröbli, the Director of the Basel University Library, for permission to research the Maurice Bavaud file in the archive of the Legal Section of the Eidgenössische Politischen Department in Bern.

11. Gerhart Hauptmann's speech at the opening of the Heidelberg Festival, in the main auditorium of the University of Heidelberg, on July 22, 1928: "Der Baum von Gallowayshire." From: Hauptmann: *Um Volk und Geist* (Berlin: S. Fischer Verlag, 1932).

12. Walter Schellenberg: *Memoirs*
Walter Schellenberg in 1939 in Venlo, Holland, which was still neutral at the time, kidnapped the two British Secret Service officers Best and Stevens, and in the process heavily wounded the Dutch general staff officer Klop, who then died. In his memoirs he testifies that Hitler immediately began to construe and construct Georg Elser, the Munich assassin, into a tool of the British. And Schellenberg was the only one to prove — which is why we print his report about the methods of "interrogation" — how and with what Elser was "worked over" so as to spill the names of his never-existing accomplices. The fact that the Gestapo and Department of Justice allowed itself so much time after Bavaud had served his harmless Augsburg prison sentence before indicting him in December 1939 speaks for his having been "worked over" by the same team of beaters that took on Elser. Why, otherwise, should he have made the most monstrous of all possible confessions?

Schellenberg writes about the interrogation of the two British officers:

Best, Stevens and the driver were taken to Berlin and then to the concentration camp Sachsenhausen. The interrogations started two days later; they were conducted by trained *Abwehr* specialists. I myself witnessed several of them and convinced myself that Best and Stevens were treated correctly. However, after Stevens once tried to commit suicide both prisoners were put in chains overnight, so that the guards would be alerted by the smallest sound to prevent a second suicide attempt. Fourteen days later when I happened to visit the camp I saw the chains. I immediately had them removed. Captain Best incidentally seems to be convinced that I stopped some letters from being forwarded to his wife. There was no way he could know that this was being done on Hitler's orders through the section that Müller headed in the Gestapo.

The results of the interrogations had to be presented to Hitler every day, who then gave his directives for the continuation of the interrogation and the treatment of the case in the press. In this it was clearly his objective to tie the assassination attempt in the Bürgerbräukeller to the activities of the secret service, in which Best and Stevens had had a hand.

The results of the investigation were turned into a summary report and showed clearly that the British Secret Service had for a long time developed a net of agents in the Netherlands against Germany which was led by Best and Stevens, and that Dutch and British intelligence had worked hand in hand. From the fact that shortly after the Venlo incident the head of the Dutch military intelligence was relieved of his command we concluded that the Dutch government regarded the collaboration between the secret services as contrary to the neutrality laws.

Best and Stevens were set free at the end of the war in 1945.

In the meantime I tried repeatedly to have them freed by way of an exchange of agents. But all my attempts failed because Himmler expressly rejected freeing these men and in 1944 forbade me to even mention it again. Hitler, he explained, still was troubled by the "failure" of the Gestapo (what was meant was the lack of success in trying to find the suspected accomplices of Elser, the Bürgerbräukeller assassin). Hitler even now suspected that Best and Stevens had known about this attempt. Himmler's last words were: "Don't bring this story up again. Otherwise the trial against the two Englishmen will take place after all."

Investigating the Beer Cellar Explosion

. . . In Berlin I found the atmosphere extremely tense. The special commission to investigate the attempt on Hitler's life had just returned from Munich. The Central Office of the Security Service was like a hornets' nest into which someone had poked a stick. The whole machinery of the Gestapo and the criminal police had been set in motion and all telegraph and telephone communications were blocked for any other business. . . .

Meanwhile a carpenter by the name of Elser had been arrested while trying to escape over the Swiss border. The circumstantial evidence against him was very strong, and finally he confessed. He had built an explosive mechanism into one of the wooden pillars of the Beer Cellar. It consisted of an ingeniously worked alarm clock which could run for three days and set off the explosive charge at any given time during that period. Elser stated that he had first undertaken the scheme entirely on his own initiative, but that later on two other persons had helped him and had promised to provide him with a refuge abroad afterwards. He insisted, however, that the identity of neither of them was known to him.

I thought it possible that the "Black Front" organization of Otto Strasser might have had something to do with the matter and that the British Secret Service might also be involved. But to connect Best and Stevens with the Beer Cellar attempt on Hitler's life seemed to me quite ridiculous. Nevertheless that was exactly what was in Hitler's mind. He announced to the press that Elser and the officers of the British Secret Service would be tried together. In high places there was talk of a great public trial, to be staged with the full orchestra of the propaganda machine, for the benefit of the German people. I tried to think of the best way to prevent this lunacy. . . .

Several days later at the Reich Chancellery, Hitler received the special detachment of the SS that had taken part in the Venlo operation. We marched into the courtyard in military formation and stood at attention while a guard of honour of the SS was drawn up in front of us. The whole thing was made into a solemn ceremony. We then marched into the Chancellery — it was the first time I had been there; the furnishings were excessively grandiose, but what I was most impressed by was the size of the rooms — and were conducted to Hitler's study, above the door of which hung a large portrait of Bismarck. Presently Hitler entered, affecting a firm, imperious stride, and placed himself in front of us as though he were about to give a command. At first he said nothing, but stared piercingly at each one of us in turn. Then he spoke. He said he was grateful for our achievement, both as individuals and as a group. He was especially pleased by our resolution, initiative, and courage. The British Secret Service had a great tradition. Germany possessed nothing comparable to it. Therefore each success meant the building up of such a tradition and required even greater determination. The traitors who would stab Germany in the back during this most decisive struggle must be ruthlessly destroyed. The cunning and perfidy of the British Secret Service was known to the world, but it would avail them little unless Germans themselves were ready to betray Germany. In recognition of our achievement and of the fact that the conflict on the secret front was just as important as armed combat on the field of battle, he would now present decorations to members of the German Secret Service for the first time in its history.

Four of the men of the special detachment received the Iron Cross, First Class, the rest the Iron Cross, Second Class. Hitler made the presentation in person, shaking each man's hand and adding a few appreciative words. Then he posted himself in front of us again in military fashion, and raised his right arm. The investiture was at an end.

We drove away in several cars while a company of Hitler's bodyguard presented arms. I must confess that at the time I was most impressed by the whole ceremony.

The next evening I was to report to Hitler at nine o'clock. Heydrich asked me to talk to Mueller before going and inform myself fully about the investigation of Elser, so that I would be able to answer any questions Hitler might ask about this aspect of the affair.

Mueller was very pale and looked overworked. I tried to persuade him that it was a great mistake to try to establish a link between Best and Stevens and Elser, and finally he agreed, but he said with a hopeless shrug, "After all, if Himmler and Heydrich cannot move Hitler on this point, you can hardly expect to be more successful. You'll only burn your fingers." I asked who he thought must be behind Elser. "I haven't been able to get anything at all out of him on that point," he said. "He either refuses to say anything or else tells stupid lies. In the end he always goes back to his original story: he hates Hitler because one of his brothers who had been a Communist sympathizer was arrested and put into a concentration camp. He liked tinkering with the complicated mechanism of the bomb and he liked the thought of Hitler's body being torn to pieces. The explosives and the fuse were given him by his anonymous friend in a Munich café." Mueller paused thoughtfully for a moment. "It is quite possible that Strasser and his 'Black Front' have something to do with this business." With his left hand Mueller massaged the knuckles of his right hand which were red and swollen. His lips were compressed, and there was a malevolent expression in his small eyes. Then he said very softly but with great emphasis, "I've never had a man in front of me yet whom I did not break in the end."

I could not repress a shudder of revulsion. Mueller noticed it and said, "If Elser had been given some of the medicine he has had from me earlier on, he would never have tried this business."

That was Mueller, the little Munich police detective, who now had practically unlimited power.

I was very thoughtful that evening as I drove to the Reich Chancellery. I reported to Himmler and Heydrich, who were there already. We stood in the ante-chamber of the great dining-room and waited for Hitler. Himmler had not yet read my report, and said he would try to read it before supper. I gave him a brief account of its contents and also of my conversation with Mueller. At the same time I reiterated all my arguments against a propaganda trial of Stevens, Best and Elser. Both Himmler and Heydrich made rather long faces. They agreed that I was right, but their problem was how to explain this to their master. Obviously, they wanted me to go ahead and try my luck.

The others present had noticed that we were engaged in a serious discussion and their curiosity was aroused. Hess, Bormann, Major-General Schmundt, and several others, came over and sought to join in the conversation, but the stony faces of Himmler and Heydrich warned them off.

Some time before this I had had a talk with Hess about Intelligence problems. This evening he showed a marked interest in me, and said to Himmler with a smile, "You know, Schellenberg and I had a discussion about political intelligence a few weeks ago. He showed me that a lawyer can sometimes have quite sensible ideas. As a matter of fact, I could use a lawyer like him myself."

Himmler merely nodded curtly, while I could see that Heydrich's ever-vigilant suspicions were immediately aroused. Indeed, the next day he asked me what I had discussed with Hess, and was not satisfied until I had repeated to him the entire conversation.

Finally the door that led to Hitler's private apartment opened. He entered, walking very slowly and talking to one of his adjutants. He did not look up until he had reached the middle of the room. Then he shook hands with Hess, Himmler and Heydrich, and finally with me. At the same time he measured me with a penetrating glance from head to foot. The others he greeted by raising his hand briefly. Then he strode into the dining-room, accompanied by Hess and Himmler.

The Adjutant quietly and quickly arranged the order in which we were to sit. On Hitler's right sat Himmler, then I, then Heydrich, and on his left Keitel and Bormann. Hess sat immediately opposite to him.

Hitler turned to me as soon as we had taken our places and said in his guttural voice, "I find your reports very interesting. I want you to go on with them." I nodded. There was a slight pause. Hitler's face looked rather red and swollen that day; I thought he must have a cold. As though he had read my thoughts he turned to me again and said, "I have a bad cold today. This low atmospheric pressure makes me uncomfortable too." Then turning to Hess he said, "Do you know, Hess, what the barometric pressure in Berlin is today? Only 739 mm. Just imagine! It's quite abnormal. It must upset people tremendously."

A subject of conversation having been found which seemed to interest Hitler, everyone began talking about barometric pressure. But Hitler now sat withdrawn and did not say a word. It was quite obvious that he was not listening.

We had begun to eat, but Hitler was still waiting for his specially prepared meal. I was very hungry and helped myself generously. Meanwhile the conversation gradually died down. It is curious, I thought to myself, no one has anything to say: they are afraid to speak.

Then the silence was broken by Hitler turning to Himmler and saying, "Schellenberg does not believe that the two British agents are connected with Elser." "Yes, my Fuehrer," replied Himmler, "there is no possibility of any connection between Elser and Best and Stevens. I don't deny that British Intelligence may be connected with Elser through other channels. They may have made use of Germans — members of Strasser's 'Black Front,' for instance — but at the moment that's only hypothetical. Elser admits he was connected with two unknown men, but whether he was in touch with any political group we just don't know. They may have been Communists, agents of the British Secret Service, or members of the 'Black Front.' There is only one other clue: our technical men are practically certain that the explosives and the fuses used in the bomb were made abroad."

Hitler remained silent for a moment. Then he turned to Heydrich. "That sounds quite possible, but what I would like to know is, what type we are dealing with, from the point of view of criminal psychology? I want you to use every possible means to induce this criminal to talk. Use hypnosis, give him drugs — everything that modern science has developed in this direction. I've got to know who the instigators are, who stands behind this thing."

Not until now did Hitler turn towards his food. He ate hastily and not very elegantly — first, corn on the cob, over which he poured plenty of melted butter, then a huge plate of *kaiserschmarren* — a kind of Viennese pancake with raisins and sugar and a sweet sauce. While he was eating he remained silent. When he had finished he said to his Aide, "I still haven't had that report Jodl was to send over."

The Aide left the room and returned about two minutes later, bringing several typewritten sheets. He gave them to Hitler and handed him a large magnifying glass. While Hitler studied the report the company round the table remained silent. Presently he said, as though he were thinking aloud, not addressing anyone in particular:

"The estimates of French steel production given in this report are quite correct in my opinion. The data on light and heavy guns — disregarding for the moment the armament of the Maginot Line — are probably also quite accurate. When I compare these figures to ours, it's quite obvious how superior we are to the French in these arms. They may still have a slight advantage in howitzers and heavy mortars, but even there we shall catch them up very quickly. And when I compare the reports on French tanks with our present strength — there our superiority is absolute. On top of this, we have new anti-tank guns and other automatic weapons — especially our new 105 mm. gun — not to mention the Luftwaffe. Our superiority is assured. No, no, I don't fear the French, not in the slightest." After having marked the report with a pencil, he handed it back to the Aide. "Put it on my desk for tonight. I want to go over it again."

To the astonishment of the others I broke the ensuing silence by asking, in relation to Hitler's last remarks:

"And how, my Fuehrer, do you evaluate the strength of England's armaments? It is quite certain that England will fight, and in my opinion anyone who does not believe that is badly informed."

Hitler looked at me for a moment with astonishment. "For the moment," he said, "I am solely interested in the strength of the British Expeditionary Force on the Continent. Our entire Intelligence Service is working on this question at present. As far as Britain is concerned, don't forget that we have the stronger air force. We shall bomb their industrial centres out of existence with it."

"I cannot at present estimate the strength of Britain's anti-aircraft defences," I said, "but we may be sure they'll be supported by their fleet, and that is certainly superior to ours."

"The support of their fleet in aircraft defence does not worry me," Hitler replied. "We shall take measures to divert the British Navy, and keep them busy. Our air force will sow mines all along the coasts of Britain. And don't forget one thing, my dear Schellenberg; I am going to build U-boats, and U-boats, and still more U-boats. This time Britain will not force us to our knees by starving us."

Then he asked suddenly: "What was your general impression during the conversations you had with those Englishmen in Holland — I mean before they were being interrogated?"

"My impression," I said, "was that Britain will fight this war as relentlessly and ruthlessly as she has fought all her wars; that even if we succeeded in occupying England, the Government and the leaders would carry on the war from Canada. It will be a life and death struggle between brothers — and Stalin will be a smiling spectator."

At this point Himmler kicked me on the shin so violently that I could not continue, while Heydrich was glaring hard at me across the table. But I could not see why I should not speak freely, even to Hitler. And as though some devil were prompting me I could not help adding, "I don't know, my Fuehrer, if it was really necessary to change our policy towards Britain after the agreement at Godesberg."

The whole company were now looking at each other, horrified by my impudence. Heydrich had paled to the roots of his hair, while Himmler looked down at the table in front of him deeply embarrassed and played nervously with his bread.

Hitler stared fixedly at me for several seconds. But I looked him firmly in the eye. For quite a while he said nothing. The pause seemed interminable. Finally he said, "I hope you realize that it is necessary to see the situation in Germany as a whole. Originally I wanted to work together with Britain. But Britain has rejected me again and again. It is true, there is nothing worse than a family quarrel, and racially the English are in a way our relatives. As far as that goes, you may be right. It's a pity that we have to be locked in this death struggle, while our real enemies in the East can sit back and wait until Europe is exhausted. That is why I do not wish to destroy Britain and never shall," — here his voice became sharp and penetrating — "but they must be made to realize, and even Churchill must be made to realize, that Germany has the right to live too. And I will fight Britain until she has come down off her high horse. The time will come when they will be ready to reach an agreement with us. That is my real aim. You understand that?"

"Yes, my Fuehrer," I replied, "I understand the course of your thoughts. But one must not forget that the mentality of an island race is different to ours. Their history and their traditions are different. They are determined by the historical laws which their insular position has imposed upon them, and as a consequence of which they are a colonial power. Theirs is the insular way of life, ours the Continental, and as a consequence of that we are now a Continental power. It is very hard to reconcile the two and quite different national characters have resulted from these differences. The English are tenacious, unemotional and relentless: it is not for nothing that they bear the name 'John

Bull.' A war like this, once it starts, is like an avalanche. And who would try to calculate the course of an avalanche?"

"My dear fellow," replied Hitler, "let that be my worry. One thing more," he said after a pause: "Have you been in touch with Ribbentrop about the Dutch note concerning the officer who died of wounds?" Then he turned to Heydrich and began to laugh. "These Dutch really are too stupid. If I were in their place I would have kept quiet. Instead they play right into my hands with this note. And when the time comes, I'll pay them back. They admit the man was an officer of their General Staff, which proves that they and not we were the first to violate neutrality."

I said that so far I had not spoken to Ribbentrop. Another pause followed. Then Hitler said to Himmler, "There are still several things I have to discuss with you." He rose abruptly, made a bow to the others at the table, and then turned to Heydrich and me. "I would like you to stay too."

We went into the next room where large easy chairs were arranged comfortably round the fireplace. On the way Himmler said to me, "You certainly are terribly pigheaded. But apparently the Fuehrer was amused." And Heydrich added, "My dear fellow, I had not realized you were such an Anglophile. Is that the result of your contact with Best and Stevens?" I realized that it would be wise to restrain myself and that I had gone about as far as I could.

For the next hour Hitler talked only to Himmler. He stood most of the time, rocking back and forth on his heels as he spoke, while Himmler close beside him inclined his face towards Hitler with an expression of rapt attention. I heard one of the SS adjutants whisper to another, "Look at Heini — he'll crawl into the old man's ear in a minute."

Hitler was drinking peppermint tea, but for his guests he had ordered champagne. After he had finished his conversation with Himmler, which had been carried on so softly that no one else could follow, Hitler turned again to the rest of the company. He spoke of the Luftwaffe, praising the work Goering was doing, and especially the fact that he availed himself of the experience of the veteran fighter pilots of the First World War. Then anti-aircraft defences, war production, and other questions of warfare were discussed. I reached home very late and completely exhausted.

The next day, at Hitler's orders, I attended a meeting between Heydrich and Mueller. The latter still looked very pale and overworked. He told us that during the night and morning three doctors, specialists in the psychiatric field, had worked on Elser and were still doing so. He had been given strong injections of pervitin, but had not changed his testimony under the drug's influence.

Mueller had also placed an entire carpenter's shop at Elser's disposal. There he had worked for the last few days and had almost completed a reconstruction of his bomb. He had also made a wooden pillar identical with the one in the Beer Cellar, and was demonstrating his method of concealing the bomb. Heydrich was extremely interested, so we went upstairs to the rooms where Elser was imprisoned.

It was the first time I had seen him. He was a small, pale man, with clear bright eyes and long black hair. He had a high forehead, and strong sensitive hands. He looked a typical highly-skilled artisan, and indeed the work he was doing was in its way a masterpiece. At first he was very shy and reserved and seemed rather frightened. He answered our questions unwillingly, speaking with a strong Swabian accent, and with the fewest possible words. It was only when we began to ask him about his work, to praise its ingenuity and precision, that he came out of his shell. Then he really came to life and went into long and enthusiastic explanations of the problems involved in the construction of the bomb and how he had solved them. Listening to him was so interesting that I completely forgot the grim purpose to which he had put all this ingenuity.

When he was asked about his two anonymous accomplices he gave the same answers as before: he had not known who they were and did not know now. Heydrich pointed out that conversations about explosives and fuses with complete strangers might be a dangerous business — hadn't he realized that? Elser replied quite unemotionally, almost lethargically, in fact, that certainly there was danger, but he had taken that into account. From the day on which he had made the decision to kill Hitler he had known that his own life would be ended too. He had been certain he would succeed in the attempt because of his technical ability. The preparations had taken him a year and a half.

We looked at each other. Mueller was quite excited, but Heydrich had a small derisive smile on his lips. Then we left.

The next day four of the best hypnotists in Germany attempted to hypnotize Elser. Only one of them succeeded; but even under hypnosis Elser gave exactly the same testimony as before.

One of these hypnotists made, to my way of thinking, the best analysis of Elser's character and motivation. He said that the assassin was a typical warped fanatic who went his own way alone. He had psychotic compulsions, related especially to technical matters, which spring from an urge to achieve something really noteworthy. This was due to an abnormal need for recognition and acknowledgement which was reinforced by a thirst for vengeance for the alleged injustice which had been done to his brother. In killing the leader of the Third Reich he would satisfy all these compulsions because he would become famous himself, and he would have felt morally justified by freeing Germany from a great evil. Such urges, combined with the desire to suffer and sacrifice oneself, were typical of religious and sectarian fanaticism. Upon checking back, similar psychotic disorders were found to have occurred in Elser's family.

Himmler was most dissatisfied with our achievements. Before going to report to Hitler he said to me, almost as though imploring my aid, "Schellenberg, this is not really our problem. What we have to do is find the people behind this thing. The Fuehrer simply will not believe that Elser did it alone, and again and again he insists on having a great propaganda trial."

It was a problem that continued to occupy Himmler for the next three months, and during that period I had the greatest difficulty in preventing Best and Stevens from being involved in the trial. [From *The Schellenberg Memoirs*, edited by Alan Bullock.]

13. Arthur Schnitzler: "März 1915," from: *Aphorismen und Betrachtungen aus dem Nachlass* (Frankfurt a. M.: S. Fischer Verlag, 1967).

14. Ingmar Bergman: Goethe Prize Speech on August 28, 1976, in the Paulskirche in Frankfurt a. M.

15. Ernst Jünger: Schiller Prize Speech on November 10, 1974, in the Neuen Schloss in Stuttgart. Already on May 6, 1945, Jünger noted down in his diary — this, too, a defense of the individual: "The number of those who suffer is meaningless — that, too, is one of those sentences through which I have unnecessarily exposed myself. But it is psychologically valid, for only the look at the individual, the one who is nearest, can open the suffering of the world up to us. It is theologically valid inasmuch as an individual can take the suffering of millions upon himself, weigh it, transform it, lend it meaning." It is

tempting to read and quote on, but I'm not at all sure whether this theological interpretation doesn't reach too far . . . into emptiness! For what do a large number of the murdered have from the fact that someone "takes their suffering upon himself." How can one do this?

16. Oswald Bumke (1877–1950) writes in his *Erinnerungen und Betrachtungen: Der Weg eines Psychiaters* [Recollections and Observations: A Psychiatrist's Way] (Munich: Pflaum Verlag, 1953) about Johann Georg Elser: "Shortly afterwards I was brought to Berlin where I had to assess the 'assassin.' There was nothing wrong with him. He was a Communist and pacifist, he declared, and that is why he wanted to eliminate Hitler and his people, because only in this way could war be avoided or quickly stopped. . . . It did not occur to me that Elser might have performed the assassination at the behest of the Gestapo. Yes, I denied it when rumors along those lines sprung up. I did not think that that much depravity was possible until I was enlightened several months after the end of the war by something that Pastor Niemöller said."

Like many others, Bumke fell victim to rumor-mongering which for decades after the liberation from the Third Reich was to deprive Elser (who was still murdered by his concentration camp beadles in April 1945 in Dachau) of his posthumous fame, until the autobiography he wrote during his imprisonment was found and published by the Deutschen Verlags-Anstalt in 1970: *Autobiographie eines Attentäters* [Autobiography of an Assassin]. In the meantime, the historian Anton Hoch of the Munich Institut für Zeitgeschichte has proved the untenability of these rumors, in whose dissemination Niemöller also participated, though accidentally, that Elser acted entirely alone during the assassination attempt in 1939 (*Vierteljahreschefte für Zeitgeschichte*, vol. 17, 1969). Unfortunately Bumke probably destroyed his irreplaceable assessment of Elser, because he regarded him — not while he was making his prognosis, but after the war because of Niemöller's claim — as nothing but a tool of Nazi propaganda. For when Dr. Anton Hoch at my behest sought to secure it from Bumke's estate he made the following discovery:

"In the meantime we have contacted the son Klaus Bumke, and Bumke's former assistant (and later testator), Dr. Stefan von der Trenck, as well as his former private secretary, Frau Alma Kreuter, and the son of his sister, Hannes Stauder. The impression we received from these conversations does not fill us with optimism. A large part of Bumke's written estate appears to have been destroyed some years ago. Otherwise, everyone disclaims knowing anything specific, and people are rather surprised by our inquiry. But I will try my luck one more time. Especially Frau Kreuter might just know more than she admits to at present. She has been rather reticent up until now. Please accept this interim report. I will be back in touch with you as soon as I have discovered more."

(A letter from Dr. Anton Hoch of the Institut für Zeitgeschichte to Hochhuth, April 14, 1975.)

The two psychiatrists mentioned in the Reich attorney general's, Dr. Lautz's, indictment of Maurice Bavaud, of November 20, 1939, concluded already during their examination that he had no accomplices: contrary to Maurice Bavaud's own assertion, which he presumably made so as to win time, until he finally admitted that he had acted entirely on his own. On page 41 of the indictment Lautz writes:

"Neither the defendant himself nor the defense cast any doubt on the defendant's accountability or sense of responsibility for his actions. On the contrary, the defendant's entire cautious, consistent and devious behavior during the execution of his plan, no less than the manner in which he responded during the judicial inquiry and during the trial to the weighty charges lev-

eled against him, showed that we are dealing with an intellectually alert and intelligent person whose complete mental accountability and sense of responsibility is legally not in doubt."
The death sentence of December 18, 1939, signed by the vice-president of the People's Court, Engert, the chairman, and by People's Court counselor Dr. Albrecht, which the Koblenz historian Oldenhage found for me, once more, on page 21, attests to Bavaud:

"Neither the defendant himself nor the defense cast any doubt on the defendant's accountability or sense of responsibility for his actions. On the contrary, the defendant's entire cautious, consistent and devious behavior during the execution of his plan, no less than the manner in which he responded during the investigative proceeding and during the trial to the weighty charges leveled against him, showed that we are dealing with an intellectually alert and intelligent person whose complete mental accountability and sense of responsibility is legally not in doubt."

17. The Federal Archive in Koblenz contains some of the files from the Reich Chancellory: R 43 II/1253. The decisive letter goes like this:

REICHSLEITER   Führerhauptquartier, 3.6.41
MARTIN BORMANN   Bo/Wn
                        Stempel: S. Ang. v. 7/6

Herr Reichsminister Dr. Lammers,
Berchtesgaden
Reichskanzlei   STRICTLY CONFIDENTIAL

Dear Dr. Lammers,
It is the Führer's wish that Schiller's drama *William Tell* should no longer be performed or taught in the schools.

I am asking you to confidentially inform Herr Reichsminister
Rust as well as Herr Reichsminister Dr. Goebbels of this matter.

> Heil Hitler!
>
> Your M. Bormann
>
> [M. Bormann]

Goebbels was evidently ashamed to execute and to pass on Hitler's order. He supressed it even though he dictated as much as
thirty typewritten diary pages a day, and devoted his special
attention to the Johann Elser assassination attempt time and
again. Goebbels had once given a Schiller memorial address,
and it appears that it did not sit well with him to have to prohibit
Tell without providing the true reasons. (For even the Swiss embassy in Berlin was repeatedly asked — after all, it could not
be ordered — to keep Bavaud's act a secret.) It did not fit at all
into the Goebbels image that posterity was to make for itself on
the basis of his diary — and which in fact it will make for itself
— if Hitler's minister of propaganda was found to be an acces-
sory to such a prohibition. For example, a year before Gerhart
Hauptmann's eightieth birthday Goebbels unashamedly remarks
that he is providing "guidelines" to desist from official celebra-
tions, and he did not show any respect for the "Goethe" of organized labor, as he called Hauptmann derisively, until after
the latter had written his song of lamentation about the incin-
eration of Dresden by the British Royal Air Force, a lament
which "well suits the poet of the Reich" (April 1, 1945). Yet
Hauptmann was not Schiller, which is why Goebbels unabashedly dictated into his diary three years before, on March
10, 1942: "I am also prohibiting a performance of *The Weavers*.
Due to its social-revolutionary character this is an extraordinar-
ily precarious subject today; a politically not entirely steadfast
director would have the opportunity to create mischief."

However, it was never to become known to the public that he, Goebbels, the "protector" of the arts, was shabbily involved in prohibiting *Tell*. Therefore, among all his entries about assassinations, after he talked to Hitler, Hess and Himmler about them, he never mentions Bavaud. He remains loyal to his experience, which is unmistakably correct, that history is not transmitted by events, as they are called, but by those who write them down — insofar as they don't "undo" these events by suppressing them. Goebbels considered this method the only correct one, as it pertained to assassinations and to his affairs with women. (On the other hand, he regarded the "Final Solution of the Jewish Question" — as he formulated it so camouflagingly — sufficiently praiseworthy to document his role as accomplice in mind and deed, though consistently avoiding the words "gassing" or "to gas.")

It is revealing that Goebbels "naturally" does not name the one and presumably only German who tried to kill him. Dismissingly once again, he hides rather than marks in his diary entry of December 19, 1942, that one of his underlings in his ministry is representing the minister at a military tribunal which sentenced a "traitor" to death who tried to blow up the bridge to Schwanenwerder together with him, Goebbels. That was Dr. Hans Kummerow, an engineer at the Loewe Radio Factory, and the fact that it had been a Ph.D., as Goebbels himself liked to be called — in contrast to all other leading Nazis, none of whom had received their doctorate — who had tried to kill him must have enraged the exceedingly vain minister even more than the "unsuitable" professions of the two Hitler assassins Bavaud and Elser, student and worker. Since Kummerow and Bavaud failed and therefore their deeds did not become public, they are never mentioned by name in the thousands upon thousands of intact pages of the minister's diary. . . .

There is no telling whether Goebbels made diary entries about Bavaud and Kummerow, say on the occasion of Stauffenberg's assassination attempt, because the diary for the year 1944 has not been found so far. However, I found no trace of the name Bavaud nor a trace of Hitler's order to Goebbels and Rust to prohibit *Tell* in the diaries from 1938 to 1945, which exist and which still lie unpublished in archives of the Hamburg publishing house Hoffman und Campe. Goebbels doubtlessly did not hear about Bavaud only from Hitler. Since he keeps delivering himself pleasurably and in the most primitive vocabulary ("Off with the noggin"), even more brutally here to his adviser Wilfred von Oven than into his diary, Goebbels as the *Gauleiter* of Greater Berlin undoubtedly received information about the goings-on in Plötzensee at the People's Court there. Goebbels's diary reveals that as of a relatively early point in time he ceased to believe in a final German victory and therefore he no longer dictated with a view to truthfulness and completeness but as a memorial, which was all that would be left of him, who in the meantime had buried his life's dream to become the historian of the Third Reich after Hitler's "Final Victory," and to use his diary as the source for his history-writing. . . .

Since Johann Georg Elser's assassination attempt had become world-renowned there was no reason for Goebbels to suppress it in his diary — but to suppress the attempts that did not become known was his principle. For example, the entry of February 1, 1940: "The children are beside themselves: the Führer is coming. He stays a few hours, plays with the children. Helga, Holde and especially Hilde are particularly sweet. We still have a chance to talk without being disturbed. I am always afraid of assassination attempts on the Führer. That would be dreadful. A few attempts were discovered in time. His private apartment in Munich is one source of insecurity. He has to have his own house in Munich. He tells me that he had constantly had premonitions of death until November 9. Now he has been seized by a firm feeling of absolute security. He must live to finish his task."

Goebbels was enough of a writer to know that what makes a journal worth reading are facts that have rarely or never been communicated and not generalities that have been noted any number of times, such as Hitler playing with children. The assassins who made a "few attempts" to kill Hitler were doubtlessly also mentioned in the course of the "couple of hours" that Goebbels and Hitler spent together, and that includes Bavaud. However, Goebbels only camouflages, fails to disclose, who these assassins are, and knows only too well how unfitting this is for the keeper of a diary. But why the reluctance? Because the fact that a Catholic seminarian wanted to kill Hitler did not fit at all into the Hitler image he wanted to give to posterity, since he himself had such an ambiguous relationship to the church. After all, he paid his tithe to his death, as did Hitler. Whereas if Bavaud had been a Jew, Goebbels would have delighted in pillorying him. But it was already sufficiently inappropriate that a German worker — Elser — had wanted to kill the chief of the so-called workers party. . . .

Goebbels was also enough of a psychologist to know that there are times when you provoke assassinations by mentioning them too often. If Goebbels is unable to pass over an assassination attempt in silence because the world press has already mentioned it, he will write: "An assassin has attempted to bomb Ambassador von Papen and his wife in Ankara. The perpetrator was totally ripped apart. Von Papen and his wife remained unharmed. . . . We are bringing the news of the assassination attempt with the corresponding commentary, but refuse to make too much of it. We believe that too much noise about assassinations can have a provocative effect in the long run. As I have already emphasized, the publication of the assassination plans against the Führer first had a shocking, then a negative effect among the people. The people don't want such news. There are certain things which should not be discussed too much in public. Among these matters are the life and health of the Führer. . . ." The minister dictated that on February 26, 1942.

With the approaching demise of Hitler Germany, Goebbels became more and more a victim of his own slogans. More and more frequently he refused to note, even in his own secret journal, what "one" — that is, the public which usually was as gullible as he regarded it — did not want to talk about. . . . Whoever leaves a diary behind has something to hide.

When the Hamburg weekly *Die Zeit* printed an excerpt from my Basel speech, I received the following letter:

Georg Ruppelt
3201 Holle 7
T. 05062/8404   Wohldenberg, December 20, 1976

Dear Herr Hochhuth!

The excerpt from your gripping and encouraging speech about Maurice Bavaud in the *Zeit* of December 17, 1976 makes me address this inquiry to you.

As a doctoral candidate who has nearly completed his dissertation about the Schiller reception in National-Socialist Germany, I am especially interested in what you say about the connection between the assassination, arrest and execution of Maurice Bavaud and Hitler's prohibition of *Tell.*

In this connection I call your attention to files from the Reich Chancellory, which reveal that Hitler already issued this edict at the beginning of June 1941; that is, just a few days after the execution of the courageous young man. (These documents will be published in January 1977 in the annual of the Schiller Society.)

My request of you, dear Herr Hochhuth, is to point out the causal connection between Maurice Bavaud's death and Hitler's antipathy to *Tell.* I will be grateful for any communication from you. . . .

With best wishes
Your Georg Ruppelt

In a study for his dissertation about the Schiller reception in Nazi Germany in the *Schiller Jahrbuch* of 1976, Georg Ruppelt proved how difficult if not insoluble the so-called Reich Minister for Science, Education and the People's Development considered the problem, on the one hand, of treating the prohibition of *Tell* as confidentially as possible and, on the other, of extending it even as far as "songs and pithy sayings" from the drama in school textbooks. This correspondence between "the secretary to the Führer," Martin Bormann, and different Berlin ministries and offices shows that Hitler himself was asked once more whether first of all it was not enough to prohibit performances of the play; second, as a school text; and third to prohibit lending it from school libraries. No, none of this sufficed for Hitler! During these the most threatening days since the beginning of the war, during the Wehrmacht's retreat from Moscow, he was still preoccupied with *Tell,* that is with Maurice Bavaud! This becomes evident from the letter which Joseph Wulf published in his documentary volume *Theater und Film im Dritten Reich* (Gütersloh: S. Mohn Verlag, 1964):

Secret
To
Herr Reich Minister for   The Reich Minister
Science, Education and   and Chief of the Reich Chancellory
the People's Development   *RK.890 Ag*
                              Berlin, December 12, 1941
                              Führer Headquarters

Re: The play *William Tell*

According to the letter of November 8, 1941 — E III a 495 g/
41 (a) — it is the Führer's wish that the play *William Tell* no
longer be used as teaching material in the schools. However,
the Führer considers it unnecessary and for technical reasons
impractical to remove the songs and pithy sayings in *Tell* from
the history and textbooks that are in use or for sale in the book
trade. New editions of such textbooks, however, should no
longer contain such pithy sayings and songs.

I have sent a copy of this letter to the chief of the Führer's
Chancellory of the NSDAP.

                                        Dr. Lammers

Hitler's directive to Bormann to prohibit *Tell*, yes, to extirpate
its every last sentence from school textbooks, triggered a jeal-
ously conducted competition among the highest Berlin party
bigwigs and authorities. The moronic pedantry and stupidity of
all this appears comical to us today. What, however, is not comical but significant and oppressive for the writing of history is
the triumph that Hitler's order to silence the Swiss student is
enjoying in posterity, even thirty years after Hitler's death! Bavaud's name appears nowhere, not in a single sentence of the
commentary to the new edition of Hitler's *Table Talk*, portions
of which, after all, were provoked by this Swiss sniper. His

name does not appear in a single Swiss or German history or biography; not in Ruppelt's documentation of the prohibition of *Tell*, which Bavaud necessitated. No, Bavaud's name cannot even be found on a plaque on his Neuchâtel birth house, not on a single street sign. . . .

Hitler intentionally never pronounced the name of Bavaud because he constantly thought of him when he was preoccupied with literature — and Schiller was the only classic that did occupy him. He prohibited *Tell* but did not bother in the least with Goethe's equally dangerous *Egmont* or *History of the Secession of the Netherlands* or about *Don Carlos* or *Wallenstein* (which Napoleon considered sufficiently dangerous to prohibit). But what all this proves is only how profoundly the man from Braunau hated this blond boy from Neuchâtel, who was quite dark-eyed but who had the right measurements to belong to the "guard" of the SS-Leibstandarte and who, even outwardly, was therefore a living embodiment of Hitler's idealistically regarded and willed "Hitler Youth." Bavaud's courage, his decisiveness, his guerrillalike slyness, his refusal to take orders from any other authority than his conscience, his ability to think for himself instead of abnegating that activity to some superior: all this made him into such an exemplary opponent that he had not only to be murdered as a person but could not even be mentioned as someone who had been beheaded.

How deeply Bavaud's act had taken root in Hitler's murderer's soul (and Golo Mann has recognized that the lust for revenge was *the* motive unique to Hitler) becomes utterly clear from Hitler's prohibition of *Tell*. It becomes somewhat less clear from his repeated perorations about Schiller's alleged mistake in having made the "Swiss sniper" the protagonist of a drama instead of looking for the material for tragedies in the German Kaiser history of the Middle Ages. But Hitler's lust for revenge expresses itself most horribly — and therefore most obscurely —

in a remark he made to Goebbels on May 8, 1943, when he stated that no one could know whether he, Hitler, would not once have his name unjustly blackened by posterity as the "butcher of the Swiss" just as present-day idiots vilified Charlemagne as the "butcher of the Saxons." Why didn't Hitler say "butcher of the Jews," which is what he was, or "butcher of the Poles"? Up until that point he had not butchered any Swiss. So far not a single Swiss except for Bavaud had opposed him. But other people had, including "Aryans" whom he proposed to "germanize" after his Final Victory. And these people had made difficulties for him, had resisted him even when they were occupied — the Danes, the Dutch, the Norwegians. But Hitler — how treacherously — did not say to his verbally nimble creature what lay closest to the tip of his tongue, what he associated most closely with the butcher of Saxons, Charlemagne: he did not say that posterity might think of him one day as "the butcher of the Danes." No, Hitler said "butcher of the Swiss" and did so presumably because he could never forget how much this *one* Swiss, Maurice Bavaud, had taught him to fear the confederates again as potential Tell descendants.